PowerPoint 365
Essentials

M.L. HUMPHREY

Individual titles, *PowerPoint 365 for Beginners* and *Intermediate PowerPoint 365* originally published and copyrighted in 2023.

SELECT TITLES BY M.L. HUMPHREY

EXCEL 365 ESSENTIALS
Excel 365 for Beginners
Intermediate Excel 365

102 Useful Excel 365 Functions

WORD 365 ESSENTIALS
Word 365 for Beginners
Intermediate Word 365

POWERPOINT 365 ESSENTIALS
PowerPoint 365 for Beginners
Intermediate PowerPoint 365

See mlhumphrey.com for more titles

CONTENTS

PowerPoint 365 for Beginners

POWERPOINT 365 ESSENTIALS - BOOK 1

CONTENTS

CONTENTS (CONT.)

Introduction

PowerPoint is a great tool if you need to present information. And it's an essential tool to learn in a number of corporate environments. I'm almost twenty-five years into my corporate career and I've yet to work for an employer who didn't use PowerPoint. These days there are sometimes other, similar options available, but PowerPoint is still that gold-standard program.

And the nice thing about mastering PowerPoint is that most of the other programs out there are based upon the same principles and concepts, so master one, you're pretty close to understanding the others.

But before we get started, we need to discuss what this particular book covers and one little issue you need to keep in mind. This book is written using PowerPoint 365 as it existed in October 2023.

All Microsoft 365 programs are a bit of a moving target because they continuously update, so your version of 365 may differ slightly.

The basics tend to stay the same so it shouldn't prevent you from learning how to use PowerPoint, but there will be changes over time.

For example, I have a different recommendation in this book about using presentation themes than I did in the original *PowerPoint for Beginners* or in *PowerPoint 2019 Beginner*. The October 2023 version of PowerPoint 365 has changed just enough to warrant that.

So I can't guarantee for you that they won't shift things again in the future. That's the risk you take using 365.

Still, the basics tend to be the basics. And the more beginner-level a book the more stable things should be. Just know that with 365 it's not set in stone the way that versions like PowerPoint 2019 are.

Another thing to be aware of is the issue of backwards compatibility. That's the ability to work with those who have an older version of the same program. If you use a tool that was just released, chances are anyone with an older version of that same program won't have the same experience you do. So when you work with a wide range of users, it is best to stick to core functions and keep it simple.

This is probably most important when collaborating with someone on creating a presentation, but it may also come up if you travel around a lot and have to present in a wide variety of settings. If you're using their computer, they may not have the same version of PowerPoint you do.

Limit yourself to the basic functionality of PowerPoint and you should be pretty safe, but it's something to be aware of. And if backwards compatibility is something you really need to keep in mind, then you may be better off learning from *PowerPoint for Beginners* or *PowerPoint 2019 Beginner*, which were written using older versions of PowerPoint. Or maybe even saving your files as .ppt files instead of .pptx files, although that may be more than you need to do.

Just keep it in mind. You should be fine, but I mention it so you're aware that it's a potential issue.

Finally, I'm going to assume here that you have worked in Word or Excel and know the basics of formatting text, etc. I will cover those topics again here just not at the same granular level of detail. If you're brand new to all Office programs, I'd recommend starting with Word first.

Okay then, let's get started by talking about how to change the appearance of PowerPoint.

PowerPoint Appearance

All of the screenshots in this book are going to be made using the Colorful theme in PowerPoint. It will look like this on the main screen when you're looking at a blank presentation:

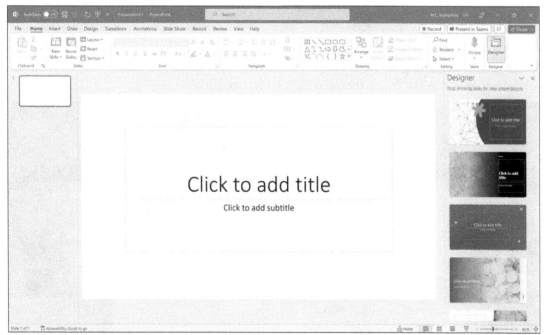

Note the orange color at the top. Also note that the background is light gray and the tasks have a white or lighter gray background behind them.

This is the Dark Gray theme:

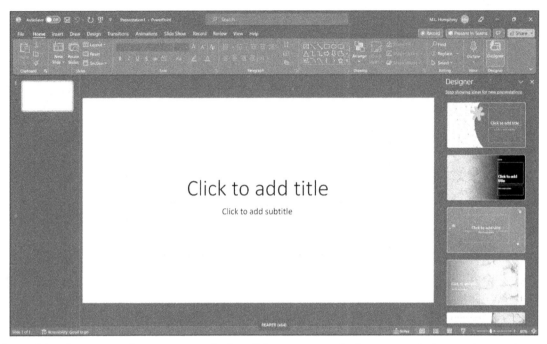

Note that the top and areas around the slide are now dark gray and the main section of options is a lighter dark gray. And that the text in those sections is white.

Another option is the Black theme which looks like this:

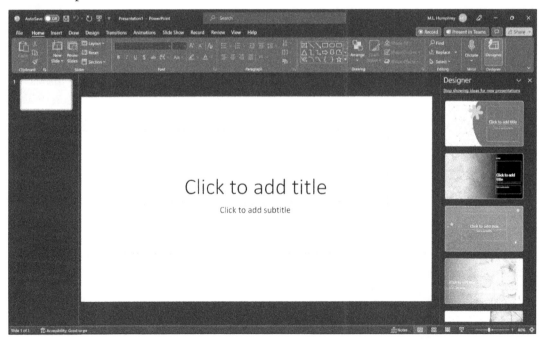

With this one, the top and surrounding areas are black and the options area is a darker gray or lighter black and the text is white.

Finally, there is a White option which looks like this:

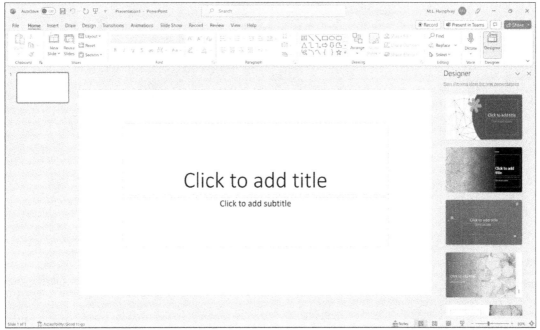

It's much the same as the Colorful option but doesn't have the orange strip across the top.

Those are the options available within PowerPoint itself, but your system settings can also impact the appearance of PowerPoint, too.

If you want your version of PowerPoint to match my screenshots, use either the White or Colorful themes, and the default system settings for Windows.

If you work with other settings, it may mean that at times I tell you something is one color when it's actually a different color for you. Do what makes you most comfortable, just keep that difference in mind.

Your office theme in PowerPoint can be changed from the Welcome screen. This should appear by default when you open PowerPoint, but if it doesn't it can also be found by clicking on the File tab from an open presentation. (Don't worry if you don't know how to do either of those, we will cover both in the Absolute Basics chapter and you can then come back here if you want to change your settings.)

The first way to change your Office Theme is to go to the Options setting at the bottom left corner of the Welcome screen and click on it:

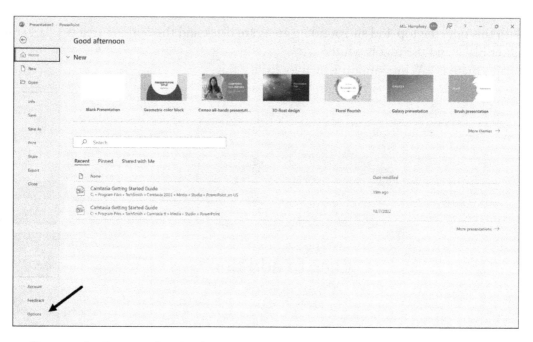

That will open the PowerPoint Options dialogue box. On the General tab under the section Personalize Your Copy of Microsoft Office, there is a dropdown for Office Theme where you can choose the theme you want:

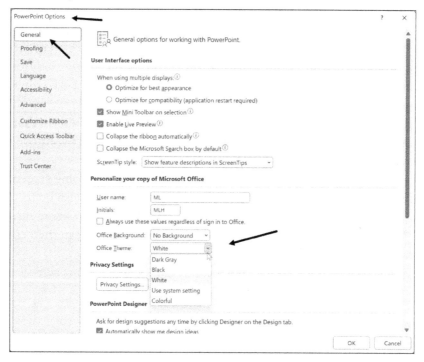

Your other option is to click on Account in the bottom left corner of the Welcome screen. That will bring up the Account page which will also have a dropdown option for Office Theme:

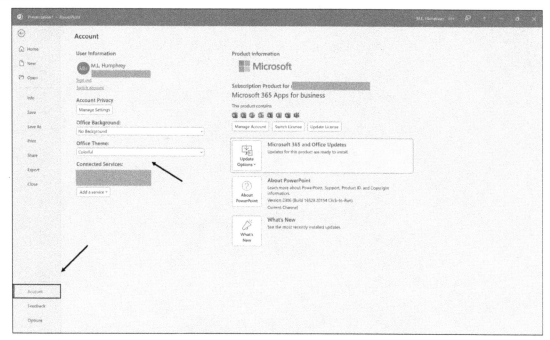

Click on that dropdown arrow and choose the theme you want to use.

Easy enough. Now let's cover basic terminology so that we're on the same page about what to call things.

Basic Terminology

Most of the terminology I use is consistent with Microsoft's Help and what others use, but some of it may be unique to me, so even if you think you know these terms, it's a good idea to at least skim this section anyway.

Tab

I refer to the menu options at the top of your PowerPoint workspace as tabs. This is because in older versions of Office when you selected an option at the top of the screen it looked like a file tab. In more recent versions of Office they've eliminated that appearance so that now the selected tab is simply underlined.

Here you can see the default tab options in PowerPoint:

The Home tab is currently selected which you can see because it is underlined. The other tab options listed there are File, Insert, Draw, Design, Transitions, Animations, Slide Show, Record, Review, View, and Help. At times in PowerPoint there will be additional tabs visible when you have certain objects selected.

Each tab has its own set of available options that are grouped together in sections.

For example, as you can see here, the Home tab includes the Clipboard section that has tasks such as copy, paste, and format paint. It also has a Slides section that includes tasks such as add a new slide, reuse a slide, change a slide layout, etc.

When instructing you on how to do something, I will tell you to go to X section of Y tab and then click on Z task. So, for example, go to the Slides section of the Home tab and click on the dropdown arrow for New Slide.

Click

If I tell you to click on something, that means to move your cursor over to that option and then use the mouse or trackpad to either left- or right-click. If I don't say which, left-click.

Left-Click / Right-Click

Left-click simply means to use the left-hand button on your mouse or to press down on the left-hand side of your track pad. (For me on my track pad, it's the bottom of the track pad, but I think some have those buttons at the top instead.)

A left-click is generally used to select something.

Right-click simply means to use the right-hand button on your mouse or to press down on the right-hand side of your track pad.

A right-click generally brings up a dropdown menu of additional options.

Left-Click and Drag

If I ever tell you to left-click and drag this just means to go to that selection, left-click and hold down that left-click while moving your mouse or cursor until you've selected all of the text, images, etc. or until you've moved that selected object to where it needs to go.

Select or Highlight

Before you can make changes to your text, such as size, font, color, etc. you need to select the text you want to edit. If I ever tell you to select text, that means to go to one end of that text, and then left-click and drag to the other end so that the text is highlighted. Like here where I have selected the text "bullet point" in the second row:

- This is a bullet point
- This is another bullet point
- This is another one

Selected text should be shaded like in the image above.

Another way to select text is to click at one end of the text you want to select, hold down the Shift key, and then use the arrow keys to select the text you want. An arrow to the right or left will select one letter at a time; an arrow up or down will select all letters between that point and the same point in the line above or below.

You can select multiple sections of text by selecting the first one normally and then holding down the Ctrl key as you left-click and drag to select the next section of text.

To select an object in PowerPoint, left-click on it. When an object is selected, there will be circles around the perimeter of the object, like this:

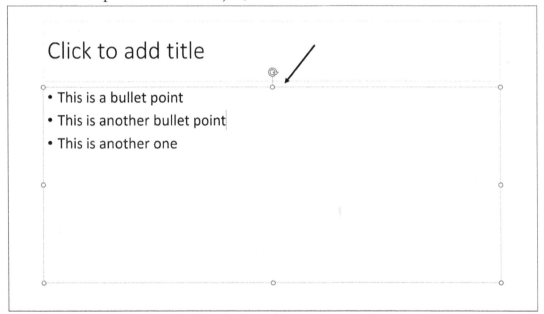

You can see that the second text box in the image above, which contains the bullet points, has been selected, because there are white circles at each corner and in the middle of each edge. Compare that to the text box above that which includes the "click to add title" text where just a faint outline is visible.

We are not going to do much with objects in this book, but I did want to mention it so you know what it looks like.

To select more than one object, click on the first object and then hold down the Ctrl key as you click on the others one at a time.

Ctrl + A, which is a control shortcut which we will define in a moment, can be used to Select All. If you are clicked into a specific text box and you use it, you will select all of the text in that text box. If you are not clicked into a specific text box, then Ctrl + A will select all of the objects on the page.

Dropdown Menu

Often there will be additional choices available if you right-click somewhere in PowerPoint. For example, if you are clicked into a text box of a presentation slide and you right-click, you will see this list of choices that let you cut, copy, paste, etc.:

I refer to this additional set of options as a dropdown menu even though sometimes it will actually drop upwards instead of downwards.

Dropdown menus can also be seen if you left-click on any of the arrows for the options under the tabs in the top menu section. For example, here is the Layout dropdown menu from the Slides section of the Home tab:

I clicked on the arrow next to Layout which brought up nine slide layouts to choose from. Anytime you see a little arrow like that next to a listed task or below it, that means there are more choices available.

Expansion Arrow

Another way to see more options in that top menu is to click on the expansion arrows that are sometimes visible in the bottom right corner of various sections. You can see one in the corner of the Clipboard section in the image above, for example. Clicking on an expansion arrow will either open a dialogue box or a task pane.

Dialogue Box

The old-school way for Office programs to show you additional options was to use dialogue boxes. Dialogue boxes appear on top of the workspace and can be left-clicked and dragged around. They are usually where you can find the most comprehensive set of options.

If you click in the bottom left-corner of the Font section of the Home tab, you can see the Font dialogue box, for example:

The Font section of the Home tab, which is visible in the background of this image, has options for font, font style, font size, font color, underline, and more. But the Font tab of the Font dialogue box includes those options as well as other options like double strikethrough, superscript, subscript, small caps, and all caps.

To close a dialogue box, click on the X in the top right corner.

Task Pane

In newer versions of Office, they tend to use what I refer to as task panes. These are separate work spaces that are visible to the sides or sometimes below your main work area.

To see an example of a task pane, right-click on a slide and choose the Format X option. It's likely going to be Format Text Effects or Format Shape depending on where you clicked.

This will open a task pane on the right-hand side of the workspace, like this one for Format Shape:

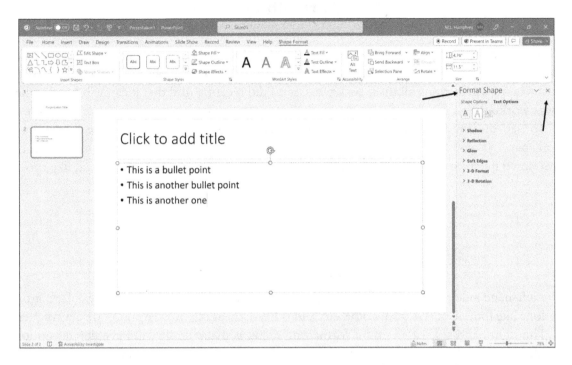

Task Panes usually have multiple sections. You can see above that this one has Shape Options and Text Options. Text Options is currently selected and has three available options to choose from, each one represented by an image with an A on it. The middle one of those is currently selected and that gives the choices of applying Shadow, Reflection, Glow, Soft Edges, 3-D Format, or 3-D Rotation to the text on the slide.

To close a task pane click on the X in the top right corner.

You can also left-click and drag to undock a task pane and move it around if you don't like the default location. To re-dock a task pane, left-click and drag to the side until it once more becomes a part of the workspace. Be careful doing this, because the task pane will reopen wherever you left it last.

Note in the picture above that there is also a sort of task pane on the left-hand side of the workspace, too, for thumbnails of the slides in the presentation. But that area can't be closed or moved. You can resize it, though, by holding your mouse over the inner margin until you see an arrow that points left and right and then left-clicking and dragging the border of the pane until it's your desired width. Note that doing this will impact the size of your slides in your main workspace, too.

You can resize any task pane that way. Just find the inner edge of the pane and then left-click and drag.

Mini Formatting Menu

If you were working in PowerPoint and following along with me, then you've also noticed something I call the mini formatting menu. It's not something I use much because it didn't exist when I was learning all these programs, but I did recently find that it came in handy when I was working on a smaller screen where the top menu options were minimized or hidden.

To see the mini formatting menu, either select some text or right-click in the main workspace. If you right-click, the mini formatting menu will appear above or below the dropdown menu of choices. If you select text it will likely appear above your text, like this:

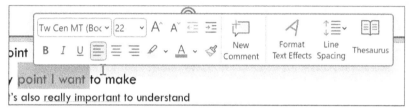

The left-hand side of the mini formatting menu includes the most common text formatting options like font, font size, font color, etc. and is fixed, meaning those options are always there.

The right-hand side of the mini formatting menu is dynamic. It will have default options like those you see here until you start working in PowerPoint, at which point those options will change to be ones you used recently.

That dynamic nature is why I don't use it often, because I'm never sure if the option I want will be there. But for basic formatting, especially if working on a smaller screen or in a tab other than the Home tab, the mini formatting menu may be the best choice.

Scrollbar

To navigate between slides in a large presentation and or through a large list of options in a dropdown menu, you will need to use scrollbars.

Here I've zoomed the main workspace so that you have scrollbars visible on both the right-hand side and the bottom. (Usually a full slide is visible so you won't have a scrollbar on the bottom.):

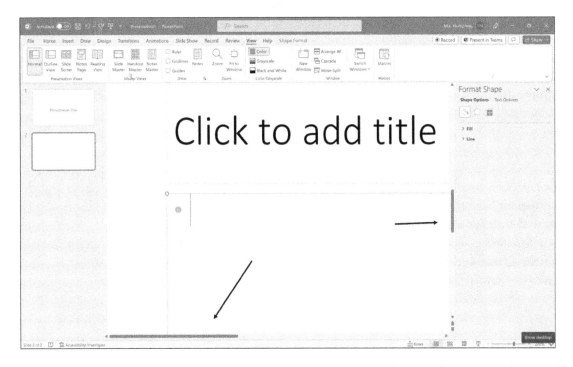

Note the dark gray bars indicated by the arrows. Those are the scrollbars. Or what I call scrollbars.

You can left-click and drag the bar itself to move quickly. In a dropdown menu, like the one for fonts, you will be able to see the choices as you do this.

In your main workspace, you will not see where you are until you let up on the left-click. But if you are scrolling down through your presentation slides it will show a small box that says "Slide X of Y" where X will change as you scroll.

(For me, scrollbars are not the best way to navigate through a presentation. I prefer to click on the slide thumbnails on the left-hand side of the workspace. But I do often need to scroll through that section when I have more than a handful of slides. That scrollbar though lets me see the slides as I do so.)

Another option for working with scrollbars is to click in the lighter-gray space around the actual bar. This will move you in that direction. So if you click in the light gray space above the right-hand scrollbar it will move you up, for example. Or if you click in the light gray space to the left of the bottom scrollbar it will move you left.

If you don't want to move that much at a time, you can also click on the arrows at the very ends of where those bars are. If you use the single arrows to navigate through your slides they will move you one line at a time if you're zoomed in or a slide at a time if you're zoomed out. The double arrows in the bottom right corner of the slide section will move you up or down one entire slide at a time regardless of zoom level.

Slider

Some options in PowerPoint use a slider, which is a horizontal bar with a perpendicular line along the bar that marks the percent value currently being used. You can see in the bottom right corner of your PowerPoint workspace the slider for your zoom level, for example. Click along that bar to change the value.

Control Shortcut

A control shortcut is when you hold down the Ctrl key (or sometimes another key) and then the specified letter to perform an action. So if I write Ctrl + C, that means hold down the Ctrl key and the C at the same time.

I will always write the shortcuts using a capital letter, like I just did, but you don't need to use the capitalized version of a letter. Just hold down that combination of keys at the same time.

Undo

This isn't really a definition, but I want you to learn it as soon as possible. If you ever do something and then regret it, Ctrl + Z will undo the last thing you did. For a more in depth discussion on using Undo and its counterpart Redo, see the Other Tips and Tricks chapter.

* * *

Okay, now let's walk through the absolute basics of working in PowerPoint, including how you open, save, and delete PowerPoint files.

Absolute Basics

Open PowerPoint

There are a number of ways to open PowerPoint. One of the easiest is to double-click on a PowerPoint file. That will open the file and PowerPoint at the same time.

Another is to go to the Start menu (bottom left corner of my screen but may be different for you) and left-click. That will bring up a large dropdown menu with pinned or recently used programs, like here where you can see PowerPoint in that first row:

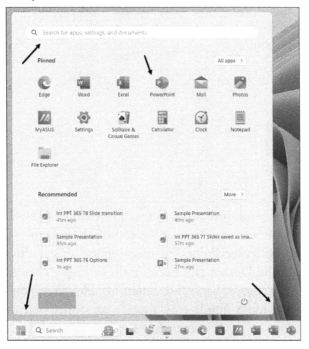

If it's there, just left-click on it.

Otherwise, use the search bar above that to find it. (As of now. They're always changing those options around a bit but the general concept stays the same. You should always see common programs and there should always be a search option somewhere.)

What I like to do is pin my most-used programs to my task bar. In the image above you can see the PowerPoint icon on the right at the bottom of the screen. Every time I need to open PowerPoint I just click on that.

To pin a program to your task bar, right-click on the icon from the start menu and choose Pin To Taskbar. You can also click and drag a shortcut to the program down to the taskbar.

Start a New Presentation

If you open PowerPoint without going through an existing PowerPoint file, you should by default open to the Welcome screen:

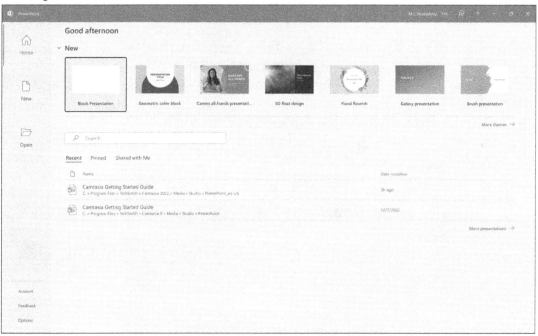

To start with an absolutely blank presentation that's just white slides with black text, click on that Blank Presentation option under New at the top of the screen.

If you're brand new to PowerPoint, I'd recommend doing this and then choosing a presentation theme from the Design tab, because those themes are easier to work with and provide a template for a more basic presentation. However, on the Welcome screen PowerPoint does also provide a number of fancier pre-formatted themes you can choose from. You can see six of those in the screenshot above.

There's also a More Themes option at the far end of that row. Click on that to see even more choices:

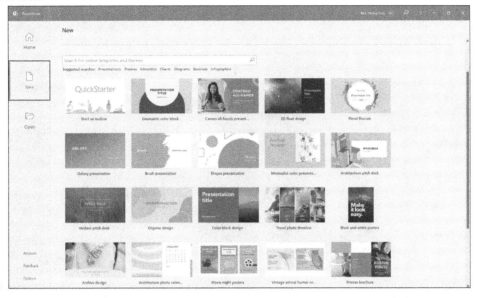

(In the image above, I scrolled down a bit to show more of the templates.)

Here we have twenty options to choose from as well as some Suggested Searches options up at the top that will give you even more choices.

To use one of those templates, click on the applicable thumbnail. PowerPoint will open a dialogue box that talks about the intended use for that particular presentation theme. Click on Create if you want to use it:

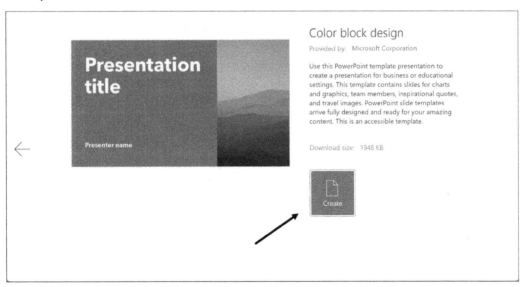

Office will then download the template for you and then open a presentation that has a number of slides visible and pre-formatted using that theme:

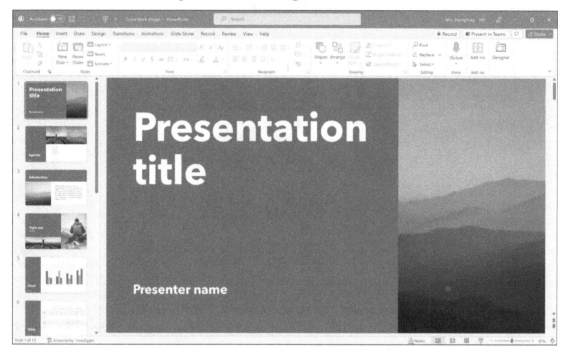

From there you can customize the presentation using your own text and images, which we will spend most of the rest of this book discussing.

If you didn't want to use that template, while you still have that dialogue box up and before you click on Create, as long as you were working from the More Themes screen you will have arrows on the left or right side of that dialogue box that you can use to move through the other template options.

* * *

If you already have a presentation open, the easiest way to start a new presentation is to use Ctrl + N. That will open a plain black and white presentation. You can then either go to the Design tab and choose a theme from there or click on one of the cover slide images in the Designer task pane that will open on the right-hand side of the workspace:

Note that the choices on the right-hand side in the Designer task pane are just a cover slide and not a fully-built template. So by default the accompanying slide layouts are going to be pretty generic. Most just have a colored background, as you can see here on the left-hand side menu of Layout choices:

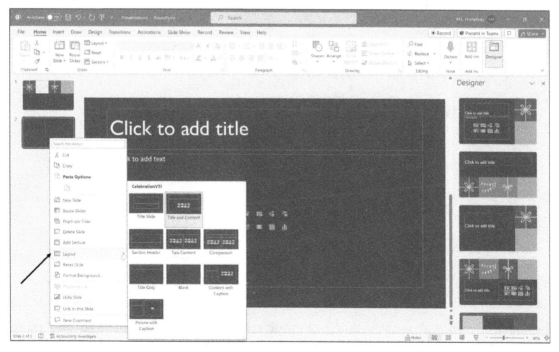

However, you can keep choosing slide layouts from the Designer task pane if you want something more interesting. As you can see on the right-hand side in the image above, Designer continues to suggest various options for each new slide layout.

Your other option for starting a new presentation when you already have one open is to go to the File tab, which will take you to the Welcome screen, and to then choose one of the presentation thumbnails from there as discussed above.

Open an Existing PowerPoint Presentation

There are two basic options for opening an existing presentation. First, go to where the file is saved and double-click to open it. Second, open PowerPoint first and then choose your presentation from there.

For the second option, if you're already working in a PowerPoint presentation, click on the File tab to get back to the Welcome screen. Otherwise, just open PowerPoint.

Your recent PowerPoint presentations will be listed in the center of the screen under Recent. Left-click on the one you want and it will immediately open.

If the file you want is not listed, you can click on Open on the left-hand side of the Welcome screen. This will bring up the Open screen which looks like this:

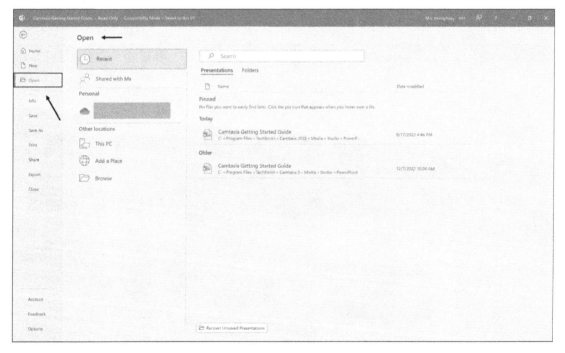

The Open screen will show a listing of your recently-opened presentations and pinned presentations on the right-hand side, but it will also have a section to the left of that where you can search on OneDrive, This PC, or click on Browse for the old familiar Open dialogue box:

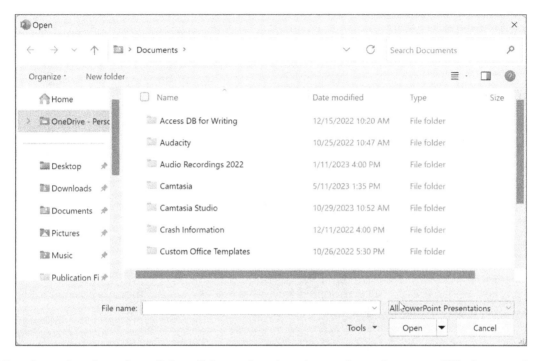

(Note here that the color of that dialogue box is going to depend on your Windows settings. I have changed my background image to a light-colored image which makes this box appear gray. When I have my default background image up instead, this dialogue box is black.)

To use the dialogue box, click on one of the folders in the left-hand side or double-click on a folder in the main section to navigate to where your file is saved. Once there, either double-click on the file you want to open, or click on the file and then click on Open at the bottom of the dialogue box.

The Open screen also has a Folders option up top that you can click on if the file you want is not one you recently opened but is in a folder you recently used. That will display a list of folder names. Click on one to see its contents and then keep clicking through to find your file. You can use the upward pointing arrow next to the file path name above the search box to go back up one level if needed:

Another option for opening a file from within PowerPoint is Ctrl + O which will take you to the Open screen.

Pin a File

If there are any presentations that you always want to be able to access quickly, you can pin them. (You can also pin folders in the same way.)

To pin a file the first thing you need to do is open that presentation. That will put it into your recent list.

Once the file is showing on the Open screen, move your cursor to the right-hand side of that listing near where the date modified is, and you'll see a pin option appear. Hold your mouse over it and it will say, "Pin This Item To The List".

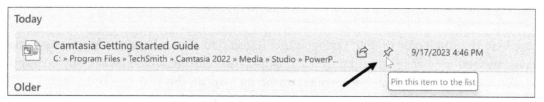

Click on that pin. The file will move to the Pinned section of your files listing and will show with a pin:

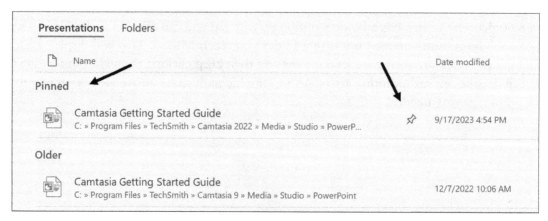

In the Open screen, pinned files are visible at the top of your file listing. In the Welcome screen you need to click on the Pinned option to see your pinned files.

To unpin a file, just click on that image of a thumbtack/pin next to the file name.

To pin a folder, it works the exact same way. Make sure the folder is listed, hold your cursor over that spot, click on the pin, and done.

Save a File

To save a file you have a few options.

Ctrl + S is one of the easiest if you want to keep working on the file. There's also a small icon of a computer disc in the top left corner that you can click on. If the file has already been saved before, that's all you need to do. PowerPoint will save over the latest version of the file using the same name and in the same location.

If the file has not been saved before and you use Ctrl + S or click on that save icon, you will see the Save This File dialogue box:

Save this file   ×

File name

Presentation title   .pptx

Choose a Location

Documents
C: » Users x

> Do you want to share this file?

More options...   Save   Cancel

There will be a default name displayed in the File Name box. It will already be highlighted, so just start typing to give the file the name you want to use instead.

Below that it will have a default location. For me it's my Users file of my C Drive. If that's fine, you just click on Save at the bottom of the dialogue box.

But if you want to use a different location instead, you can click on that dropdown arrow and choose from the listed options. Or you can click on More Options in the bottom left corner. That will take you to the Save As screen:

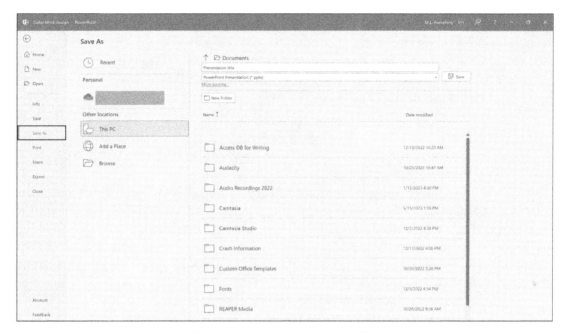

The Save As screen is going to list a larger number of possible folders to save to and also let you change the file type if you need to do that.

You can click on Browse from the Save As screen to bring up the Save As dialogue box which will also let you choose a location, name, and file type.

For most presentations that have been saved before, you'll just save using Ctrl + S or that icon in the top left corner. You can even just close the presentation and when PowerPoint asks if you want to save your changes say yes.

But there are going to be times when you want to save a file with a different name or different format. When that happens, click on the File tab and then click on Save As on the left-hand side of the Welcome screen. From there you can change whatever you need to change.

Do be careful though about changing things this way. If you just wanted to move a file to a new folder, it's better to do that outside of PowerPoint. Same with renaming the file. Let's talk about that now.

Move a File

If you want to just move a file from Folder A to Folder B, that is best done outside of PowerPoint. Close the file, go to the folder where it is saved, select that file, Ctrl + X to cut it from its current location, go to where you want the file to move, and Ctrl + V to place it in that new location.

Keep in mind that if you move a pinned file or a file that was in your recent files list, you will no longer be able to open it from those lists in PowerPoint, because PowerPoint will go to the old location looking for the file and it won't be there anymore. (Same goes for when you change the name of a file.)

Rename a File

If you want to change the name of a file but don't want multiple versions of the file to exist, that should also be done outside of PowerPoint. Find the file where it is saved, click on it to select it, click on it again to make the name editable, and then make your name change. Hit Enter or click away when done.

Delete a File

Deleting a PowerPoint file also needs to happen outside of PowerPoint. Find the file where it's saved, right-click and delete. Or click on it and choose the trashcan or delete option at the top of the dialogue box.

Close a File

Okay. Back to PowerPoint.

The easiest way to close a presentation is to click on the X in the top right corner of the PowerPoint workspace. If you had a single presentation open that will also close PowerPoint.

If you have multiple presentations open that should just close that presentation.

If the presentation you try to close has unsaved changes, PowerPoint will ask if you want to save those changes before closing:

Save will save those changes with the same name, file location, etc. and will replace the prior version of the presentation.

Don't Save will close the file without keeping any of your changes from this session.

Cancel will keep the file open. Choose Cancel if you're not sure and want to review the document before closing it or if you want to use the Save As option to save a new version and keep the old one untouched.

To close a file you can also go to the File tab and then choose Close from there.

Or you can use Ctrl + Q to both save and close a presentation or Ctrl + W to just close a presentation.

Personally, I like to be reminded that there were changes made to my presentation before I close it so I'd avoid using Ctrl + Q, because it never fails that you realize you didn't want to save those changes about three seconds after you automatically save them. But it's there if you want to use it.

* * *

Okay. Those were some of the absolute basics of working with files in PowerPoint. Next let's discuss how to choose a presentation theme from within a new presentation and then we'll cover the layout of your workspace.

Presentation Themes

We've touched on these a bit already, but I wanted to devote a full chapter to presentation themes, because as a new user of PowerPoint I highly recommend working with an existing presentation theme. They often come with a variety of slide layouts that are already formatted for you, and they tend to have nice accent elements that a plain, black and white presentation doesn't have.

We already covered the themes available on the Welcome screen, but I don't recommend those for new users. They're a little too fancy and it's a little too easy to get stuck trying to adapt one to what you need as a new user.

Instead, I recommend that new users start with the black and white presentation option and then go to the Themes section of the Design tab:

You can see here the current theme as well as eight other choices. In the bottom right corner of that row, there is a downward pointing arrow with a line above it. Click on that to expand your list of choices.

To see how each theme will look, hold your mouse over the option. To select a theme, click on it.

The nice thing about using one of these themes is that moving back and forth between them is relatively easy. You just click on the one you want and everything updates.

Many of the theme choices in this section also have variants. You can find them in the Variants section of the Design tab after you click on a theme.

So here, for example, the Facet theme has a green, a blue, and a pink option as well as a version that uses a dark green background:

There is also a Colors dropdown that you can find if you expand the variants section. Expand that section and then hold your cursor over Colors and a secondary dropdown menu will appear with a large list of color combinations to choose from.

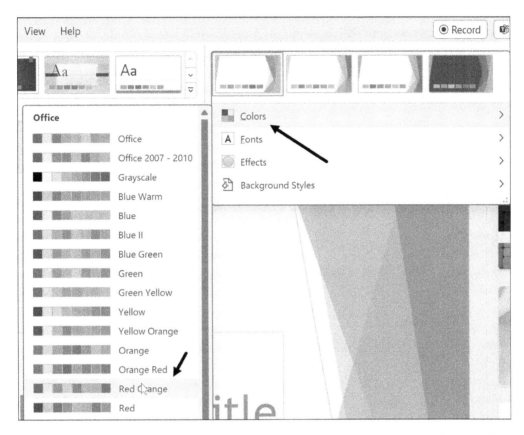

Click on the color combination you want to use. Above, for example, I applied a Red Orange color palette to the Facet theme and you can see in the background that the accents and text changed to match that choice. (In print, maybe not, but in the ebook you can see that.)

For a beginner, I think there's plenty here to work with and it's pretty forgiving, too, so I strongly urge you to use one of these themes for your presentation if you don't have a corporate one you need to use.

The problem I found with using the themes currently listed on the Welcome screen is that when you try to change to a theme in the Themes section of the Design tab, at least for the few I tried, PowerPoint didn't completely change over. It combined the two themes, and not always in a good way.

As a beginner, I wouldn't expect you to be able to unravel that. So to avoid that potential complication, I'd say just start with a blank presentation and then choose an option from the Design tab.

(This is different, by the way, than earlier versions of PowerPoint where the Welcome screen choices corresponded to the Themes options on the Design tab. So it may change back in the future. But for now, save yourself the heartache.)

Also, even though they don't show up by default when you choose a theme, all of these older design choices do come with a variety of built-in slide layouts that use those colors and design elements. Here, for example, Facet has fourteen different slide types for you to choose from.

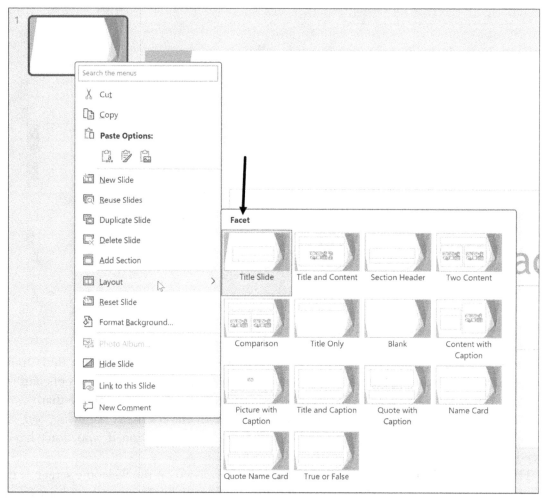

All of those layouts use the same font, color, and accent elements to help you create a cohesive presentation. Is it sexy? Nah, not really. Is it functional? Yes.

Okay. So that's my advice. Open a black and white presentation, choose a theme from the Design tab, and change the color if you want to be adventurous.

But. When you open a black and white presentation, PowerPoint is also going to open the Designer task pane on the right-hand side. Like so:

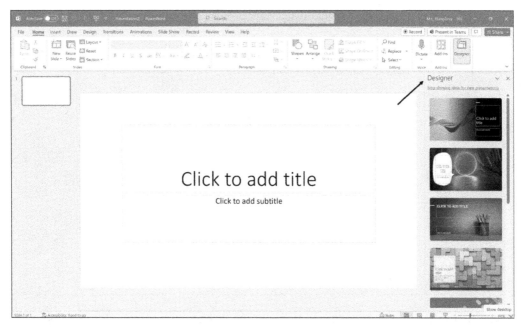

My advice is to ignore it. Click on the X in the top right corner and pretend you never saw it.

But if you're tempted…you can click on one of those options in the task pane and PowerPoint will apply that design to your title slide. If you're lucky it will also offer you some good layout options for other slides in your presentation.

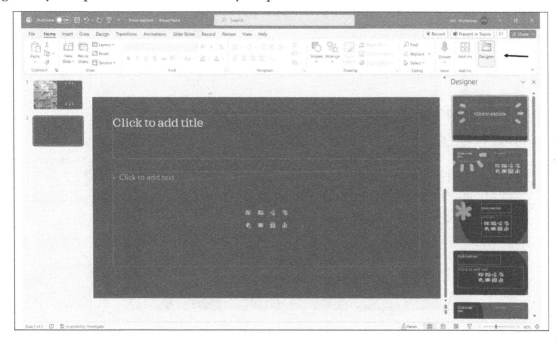

If you're not, you'll get options like this:

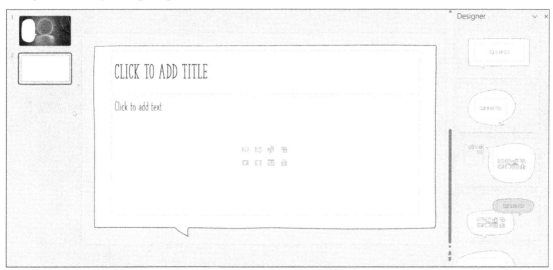

And switching over after you've made that choice is not easy to do. Best to just close the presentation and try to start again instead of try to choose another option.

Now, I understand that you may not be thrilled with using those basic presentations in the Themes section of the Design tab. Another option to make things more interesting, is to start with one of the basic themes, add a new slide (we'll cover how to do that soon), and then open the Designer task pane to see more layout choices than the default. Like these:

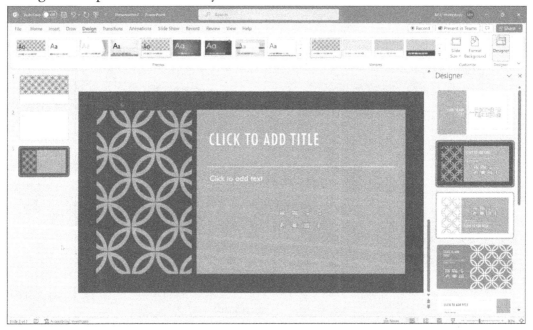

To open the Designer task pane, click on Designer in the Designer section of the Design tab, which you can see in the top right corner of the image above.

I think that gives workable options that are maybe a little more interesting than the default and that still work thematically. You can also switch to a new theme without PowerPoint trying to combine the two designs, although be forewarned that you'll probably have to go through each slide and choose a better layout option.

So that's probably your best call. Start with a blank presentation (Ctrl + N or click on that option on the Welcome screen), apply a theme from the Themes section of the Design tab, choose a variant or color option, if wanted, and then click on Designer to give yourself more choices for your slide layouts.

But only click on Designer after you've added at least one slide to your presentation, don't use it on your title slide.

And one final note. If you move to a new theme after you've added text to your presentation, be sure to check all of your slides. Sometimes there will be a difference in font size or font choice that impacts your appearance. Also be especially careful if you were using a theme that had all caps in the title sections and you move to one that uses upper and lower case. I often find that I didn't properly capitalize my words when all caps was in place.

One more thought. If you are going to print your presentation, try to find a presentation theme that has a white background on the main slides. Like this one:

It is possible to set your print settings to address slides with dark backgrounds when it comes time to print, but I always prefer that my presentation on the screen match what I've printed.

The reason not to print slides with a dark background is that it takes a lot of ink. And sometimes, depending on the type of printer, a dark background has more chance to smear or smudge or come through stripey.

Also, make sure the theme you choose has layouts that meet your needs. Are there section slides if you need that? Are there image slides? What about the bulleted lists, do they work for you? It's far easier to start with a theme that is set up for your needs than to try to edit it later. And in this beginner book we're not going to cover too much about how to make those sorts of edits, so you're going to be stuck with how the theme is set up.

Okay, now let's look at your workspace.

Your Workspace

This is what PowerPoint looks like using a presentation that has about a dozen slides:

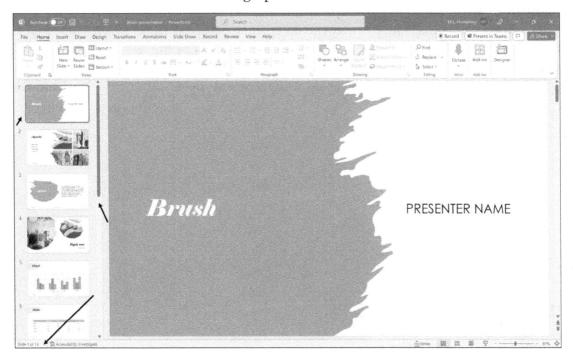

As discussed previously in the definitions section, across the top of the workspace are the tabs, File, Home, Insert, etc. You can click on each of those to see the available options and then click on an option to apply it.

Below that, on the left-hand side of the workspace, are thumbnail images of each slide. You can see six slides at a time at the current size. On the bottom left corner it shows that there are a total of 13 slides in this presentation. The scrollbar for that section is on the right-hand side of the thumbnails, and can be used to move down to see the rest of the slide thumbnails.

To the right of that is the main part of the workspace where you can see the current slide and then to the right of that is another scrollbar.

There is a slider in the bottom right-hand corner of the workspace that will let you zoom in or out on the current slide. My default zoom percentage is 97% which usually lets you see the entire slide while keeping the slide thumbnails visible on the left-hand side. I tend to leave this on the default setting but you can click down there to change your zoom level quickly.

In the image above, I am clicked onto Slide 1. You can see this in the left-hand set of thumbnails where there is a darker border around Slide 1 and the number of the selected slide is also a different color.

To move to a different slide in the presentation, either left-click on a slide thumbnail in the left-hand section, or use the scrollbar on the far right of the currently-visible slide. In that far right scrollbar the double arrows in the bottom right corner will move you one slide at a time regardless of zoom level.

As you work in PowerPoint you may end up opening other task panes which will appear on the right-hand side of the current slide or below it. Or even to the left if you change your settings. But what you see above is the core appearance that you'll see most often.

Now let's walk through what you can do with those slide thumbnails on the left-hand side.

Slide Thumbnails Task Pane

As we just discussed, the left-hand side of your workspace shows thumbnail images of each slide in your presentation. This is where you go to add, delete, or move around your slides in your presentation.

Add a Slide

If you want to add a slide to your presentation, there are a few options available to you.

You can right-click on the slide directly above where you want to add that new slide and choose the New Slide option from the dropdown menu:

That will add a blank slide that corresponds to the template you're using. The layout used will vary depending on the slide that was directly above.

Here I right-clicked on the top slide for this presentation style and chose New Slide and it added a slide in the default layout for this template as Slide 2. But then I also did the same on what is now Slide 3 and it added a new slide in the same layout as Slide 3 as Slide 4:

So. The layout you'll see on your new slide is going to vary depending on where you insert the slide and what layout was being used above that. (But, as we'll discuss momentarily, you can easily change that.)

Another option for inserting a new slide is to go to the blank space at the very end of the Presentation Slides Task Pane and right-click on that space. Choose New Slide from there and

PowerPoint will add a slide to the end of your presentation using the same layout as the last slide.

Your final option is to go to the Slides section of the Home tab and click on New Slide. If you use the dropdown arrow under New Slide, you can choose the layout you want:

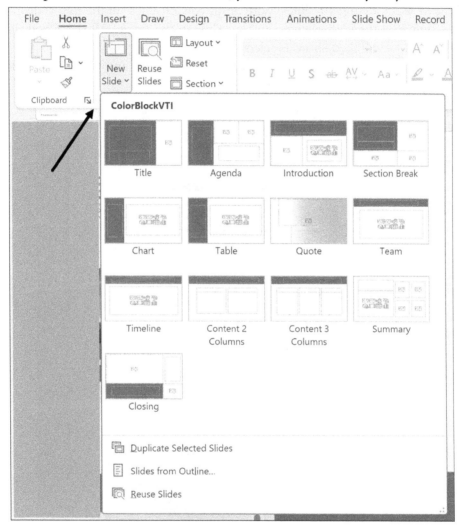

Simply click on your preferred layout from that dropdown. The new slide will insert below the slide you currently have selected in the presentation. If no slide is selected, it will insert at the end of the presentation.

Select Slides

To select a single slide, just left-click on it.

To select multiple slides, left-click on the first slide, and then either hold down the Shift key or the Ctrl key and select the next slide.

Use Ctrl if you want to select one additional slide at a time and also if the slides you want to select are not next to one another.

Use Shift to select a range of slides. With Shift, you left-click on the first slide in the range, hold down Shift, and then left-click on the last slide in the range. All slides between the two slides you clicked on will then show as selected.

Selected slides have a darker border around them and the number of the slide is also a different color. Here I have selected slides 1 through 3:

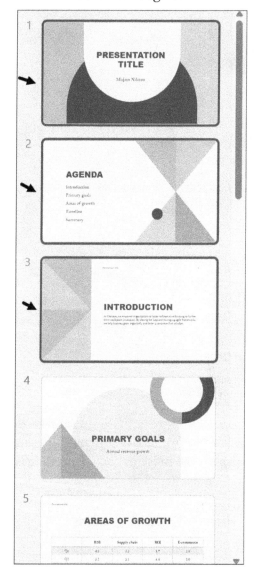

I clicked on Slide 1, held down Shift, and then clicked on Slide 3. (I could have also held down Ctrl and clicked on each individual slide, but Shift saves time when you're selecting a range of slides at once.)

You can combine Ctrl and Shift together to select slides. So maybe you use Shift to select three slides that are next to each other and then Ctrl to select one more slide that isn't next to those three.

To go back to just one slide selected, click on that slide.

You can also click into the gray area at the bottom of the task pane if you don't want any slides selected. The slide you'll see in the main workspace in that case will be the last one in the presentation.

If you want to select all of the slides in the presentation, click into the Presentation Slides task pane, and then use Ctrl + A.

Move a Slide or Slides

It's not a problem if you insert a slide in the wrong location. You can easily move the slide to where you need it. You can also move a range of slides at one time.

To move a single slide, left-click on the slide you want to move, and then hold that left-click as you drag the slide to its new location. Release your left-click when you reach your destination.

Here you can see that I've left-clicked on Slide 18 and am dragging it upward past Slide 17:

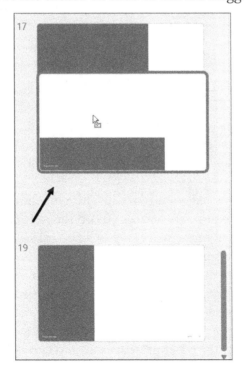

As it reaches a spot above Slide 17, Slide 17 will shift downward to make room for that slide to go above.

To move multiple slides at once, it's basically the same, you just need to select all of the slides you want to move first, and then left-click and drag.

Here you can see that I'm moving two slides (see the red 2 above the outlined slides) and that I've moved those two slides to a spot between the existing Slides 5 and 6 (see the slide numbers on the left-hand side):

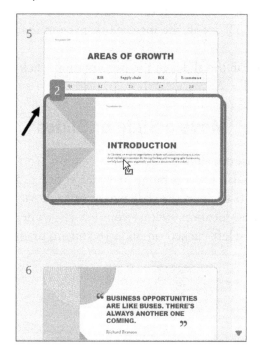

Note that as you moves slides around they will not keep their numbering. The numbering is based on that slide's current position in relation to all of the other slides in the presentation. As soon as you move your slides into their new location, all slides in the presentation will renumber to adjust to their new position.

You can also Cut and Paste a slide to move it. This sometimes is the easier option if you want to move a slide a large number of spaces. To do this, left-click on the slide you want to move, use Ctrl + X (or click on the scissors in the Clipboard section of the Home tab), go to the place in the presentation where you want to place the slide (using the scrollbar on the right-hand side of that task pane if needed), click on the slide above where you want to place the slide, and then use Ctrl + V (or the Paste option in the Clipboard section of the Home tab) to paste the slide into its new location.

Cut can also be used to take slides from one presentation to another. Select the ones you want to move, Ctrl + X, go to the other presentation, and Ctrl + V.

If you want the slides that you paste into the second presentation to use the formatting of that second presentation, then use the Paste dropdown menu in the Clipboard section of the Home tab to choose a different paste option. There are three options to choose from:

You want the first option, Use Destination Theme.

You can see the description of each paste option if you hold your mouse over the little icon. Right now the Use Destination Theme option looks like a clipboard with an "a" in the bottom right corner with dots under it.

You can also find these paste options when you right-click in the gray space of the Presentation Slides task pane. Either one will work.

Cut, or Ctrl + X, takes a slide from where it is and moves it to a new location. But if you want a copy of that slide to move and want to keep the original where it is, then use Copy, or Ctrl + C, instead. Everything else works the same in terms of pasting the slide into its final location, but Copy will leave the original slide where it was.

In the Clipboard section of the Home tab, Copy is represented by an image of two pieces of paper stacked on one another.

(Note that sometimes Microsoft decides they need to refresh the look of their product and changes the appearance of these icons. But they generally stay in the same location. And in twenty-five years they have yet to change the Ctrl shortcuts. So if you know the Ctrl shortcuts you should always know a way to cut, copy, and paste.)

Duplicate a Slide

PowerPoint also has an option similar to Copy which is Duplicate. You can find it by right-clicking on a slide thumbnail or by using the dropdown under the Copy option in the Clipboard section of the Home tab.

Duplicate takes the slide you currently have selected and puts an exact copy of that slide directly below. So it saves that step of having to paste.

It will copy any text or images, etc. that were on the source slide so if a header is going to stay the same or you have other elements that will repeat from slide to slide, it's very useful.

And you can use it on more than one slide. Just select the slides you want to duplicate first and then choose the Duplicate option and all of the selected slides will be duplicated.

Delete a Slide

To delete a slide, right-click on it and choose Delete Slide from the dropdown. This also works with multiple slides at a time.

Another option is to use the Delete key when you have a slide or slides selected. The Backspace key also works to delete a selected slide or slides.

Reset a Slide

If you make changes to a slide and you don't like them and you want to go back to the default format for that theme, you can reset the slide. Right-click on the slide and choose Reset Slide from the dropdown menu or go to the Slides section of the Home tab and choose the Reset option from there.

When pasting in slides from another presentation, even if you pasted in using the destination theme, you may still want to do this. When I just did this with my pasted slides it brought my text to a left-aligned position instead of centered, for example. If I'd already had slides in this presentation that had been created in the presentation, that difference in alignment would have been noticeable and needed to be fixed.

* * *

Next let's discuss how to choose slide layouts.

Slide Layouts

A good presentation will vary the appearance from slide to slide. Maybe one slide will just contain text but then another will have a chart or two columns of text side-by-side. Presentation themes often have these various layouts built in so that you don't have to try to create one on your own.

To change the layout of a slide, right-click on either the slide thumbnail in the Slide Thumbnails task pane or in the main workspace. Next, go to the Layout option. There should be a secondary dropdown menu that shows you the available layouts for that presentation theme:

Click on the one you want to use.

You can also do this by selecting the slide and then going to the Layout dropdown menu in the Slides section of the Home tab. Just click on the arrow next to Layout and choose from there.

If you're using the Designer task pane, you can also click on one of the options shown there to apply it. The Designer task pane will not always have suggestions for all slide types, though.

Also, not all themes will have all layouts, so be sure to check what choices you have available before you start working with your chosen theme.

Now that you know how to apply a layout, let's discuss some of the more common choices.

Title Slide

The title slide is the first slide in your presentation. It will usually have a space for a title and a space for a subtitle as well as the design elements for your chosen theme.

Here, for example, is the title slide for the Facet theme:

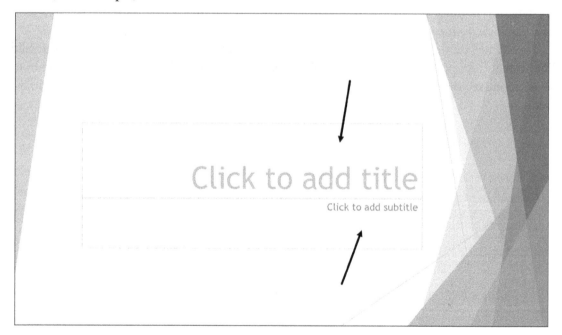

It places the title and subtitle in the center of the slide.

Other themes will place those elements in different locations. For example, the Frame theme places the title and subtitle on the left two-thirds of the slide.

Section Header Slide

Another common slide layout is the Section Header layout. It usually includes fields for a title and a sub-header:

Often-times this will look very similar to the title slide, but maybe the colors on the slide, the font size, or the placement of the text or design elements will differ slightly.

With this theme, the text is on the left of the page instead of centered and the design element in the background is different on the left-hand side.

The Section Header slide is one where you might want to use the Designer to choose different options. In this case there are options with a dark background, like the first and third options here, that make the section stand out more:

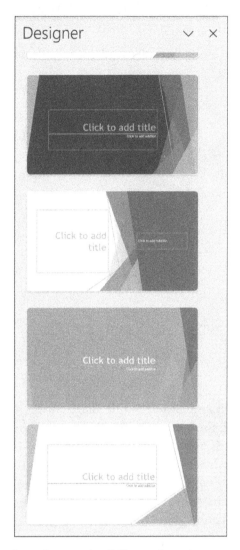

There are also choices that place the text in different locations on the slide, like in the second option.

Remember, if the Designer tab is not visible you can open it by clicking on Designer in the Designer section of the Design tab. Scroll down to see all of your options.

One caution about using the Designer is that the list of slide choices is not going to be the same each time. So if you choose a design that you like for one section header, you'll likely need to duplicate that slide for your next section header to use it again.

Title and Content Slide

The Title and Content Slide is your bread and butter slide. This is the one you will probably use the most. It has a section with the title for the slide, which is usually what that slide is about, and then another section where you can add text or another element like a video, image, illustration, graph, or chart. (We're only going to cover adding text in this book but the Title and Content slide will accommodate any of those other elements, too.)

This theme uses a pretty standard layout with the title at the top and then the text or other element below that. But, as we can see with the Designer choices, that's not the only way to go. Some themes put the title on the left and text on the right like the fourth option here:

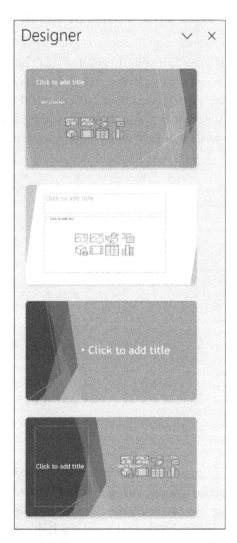

Also, if using Designer, be careful, because as you can see here, sometimes the suggested layout doesn't match the type of slide you want, like in the third example there that only has a title.

Two Content or Comparison Slide

A Two Content slide generally has a title section and then two sections with text or other elements side-by-side.

This is one that, at least for this theme, PowerPoint didn't have additional suggestions for in the Designer tab. If I wanted something different then this basic appearance, I'd probably have to build it myself. Not a beginner-level skill.

A Comparison slide layout is much like a Two Content slide, but it has one additional text box above each of the sections in the main body of the slide so you can label those contents.

Content or Picture with Caption

A Content With Caption slide has a title section and an associated text box, and then another box for text or another element like a picture, video, etc.

This is a good one for a high-level description, a descriptive paragraph, and then an image, like this:

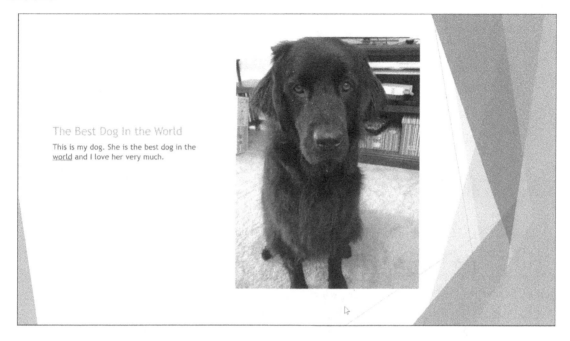

A Picture With Caption slide is similar but may limit the choice for that third box to just a picture as opposed to text or images. Also, the positioning of the three elements may differ between the two different layouts.

* * *

There are a number of other slide types, but the ones above are probably going to be your core group of slides. Once you've selected a theme to work with, you can look at the layout choices and see if any of them will fit for what you want to do. For a basic presentation, you should be fine no matter what theme you choose.

Okay. Now that you know the basics about working with your slides and applying a layout to them, let's talk about how to add and format text, which is usually the core of creating a PowerPoint presentation.

Add, Move, or Delete Text

Add Text

It's very easy to add text to a PowerPoint slide. Find a text box, click on it, and start typing. That's why I recommend using the theme templates, because they already have text boxes for you and they're generally located in good spots on the slide.

So, how do you know where a text box is? Simple. They usually say something like "Click to add title" or "Click to add subtitle". Like here:

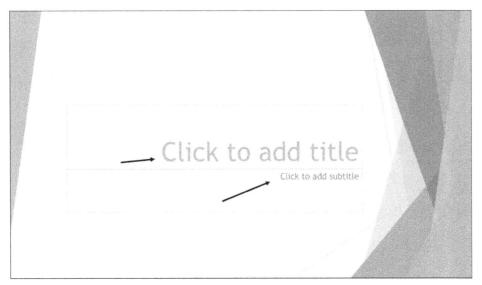

You can see the boundaries of the text boxes with that faint gray line around the edges. The current text color, font, and size is what your text will look like when you click into the box and start typing.

You don't have to replace that text "click to add..." because it will disappear as soon as you click into the text box. (If you already had text in a text box, then, yes, you would have to delete that text to get rid of it, but not this placeholder text.)

When you're done typing your text into the text box, click away from it. The outline of that text box will go away and you'll just have your text. Like so:

All slides work this way. Some, though, are going to have bulleted lists. Like this one:

In that case, when you start typing and hit Enter for a new line in that main text box, it will put bullet points at the start of each line. Use the Tab key to indent a line of text and create a multi-level bulleted list. Like so:

> A Really Important Point
>> No, seriously, very important
>>> The most important point of all
> A Second Really Important Point
>> But maybe not as important as the first one

To enter this text, I clicked into the text box, typed the first line, hit Enter, used Tab, typed the second line, hit Enter, and used Tab again before I typed the third line of text. That gave me the first three lines.

I then hit Enter and used Shift + Tab twice to move the bullet point back to the first level, and then added that line, Enter, Tab, and then the final line of text.

So with bulleted lists, Tab will move the bullet point in one, Shift + Tab will move it back one. It's easiest to do as you type, but if you need to make adjustments later, click into the line of text right before the first letter, and then use Tab or Shift + Tab as needed.

Another option is to click anywhere on a line and then go to the Paragraph section of the Home tab and use the Decrease List Level or Increase List Level options:

In this template, the various indented text levels had text that was smaller with each indent, but the bullet point remained a green arrow. In other templates the type of bullet point used may change with each level.

As a beginner, I would suggest letting PowerPoint set those shapes and text sizes. These templates tend to be built for use as a presentation that will be shown on a projector screen, so they won't use too small a font size to be visible in that setting. See here how the text in the last three bulleted lines is the same:

> ▷ A Really Important Point
>
> ▷ No, seriously, very important
>
> ▷ The most important point of all
>
> ▷ It really is
>
> ▷ I'm not lying
>
> ▷ This is really, really, really important|

One final comment, if you're working in a company presentation template and having issues with the bulleted lists not working, that's probably an issue in the master slide of the template, and you'll need someone to fix that or you'll need to switch to a different template or presentation theme. So sometimes it's not you, it's them.

Move Text

You move text in PowerPoint in the same way you would in Word, which I hope you're familiar with already.

Select the text you want to move, and then use Ctrl + X or go to the Clipboard section of the Home tab and click on the scissors to cut the text from its current location. Next, click on where you want to place that text, and then use Ctrl + V or the Paste option in the Clipboard section of the Home tab to place the text.

You can also select the text and then right-click and choose Cut from the dropdown menu, go to where you want to place the text, right-click, and choose Paste from the dropdown menu.

Copy Text

Usually you'll want to move text not copy it, but you can copy using Ctrl + C, the Copy option in the Clipboard section of the Home tab, or by right-clicking and choosing Copy from the dropdown menu. Just select your text first. The text will remain where it is, but you can then also go to a new location and paste that text there as well.

Paste Options

As mentioned above, there is more than one paste option. Either click on the arrow under Paste in the Clipboard section of the Home tab or right-click to see the list of paste options.

We already discussed the first option there, Use Destination Theme. That makes sure the text fits in with what's around it in terms of font, color, etc.

The next one is Keep Source Formatting which will paste the text in but keep it the same color, font, etc. that it was when you copied it.

The third option, Picture, pastes the text in as a screenshot. The text won't be editable at that point. It will be as if you'd taken a photo of that text and dropped in the photo.

The final option, Keep Text Only, will format the text depending on the text that's around it. Here's an example of all four options:

My source text was in green and used the Trebuchet MS font. The presentation I'm pasting into uses the Garamond font in black, like in that first bulleted line there.

In the second bulleted line, I pasted in "THIS IS THE BEST" using the Keep Text Only option. I did the same thing for the last line of text. Note how different they are.

That's because the first line was pasted directly after a line that had black text in Garamond and the second one was pasted directly below a line that had green text in Trebuchet MS.

Each one used the formatting of the text immediately before it.

The third bulleted line in the image above was pasted in using Use Destination Theme. No matter where I pasted that text in within that text box it was going to look like that.

The fourth line is that same text pasted in using Keep Source Formatting. It continues to look like the text I initially copied, which was green and in Trebuchet MS font.

Finally, down there in the center bottom you have a picture of the text I was copying and pasting. I can't edit the text in that last one, it's a picture at this point. And it doesn't position like text anymore either. I have to click and drag that image around to place the text on my slide. But that is a true image of what the source text I started with looked like.

Delete Text

To delete text, select the text, and then use Backspace or Delete.

If you don't select the text first, you can remove text one character at a time. Delete will delete the character to the right of your current position. Backspace will delete the text to the left of your current position.

Delete and Backspace also work on bullet points and the numbers in numbered lists.

Design Principles

Feel free to ignore this section. I have given a number of presentations to various audiences over the years and been on the receiving end of even more, but at the end of the day I have no formal design training, this is just what I've picked up in my finance/consulting/corporate career.

Font Size

For a presentation that is going to be given as an actual presentation, I prefer to keep the font size to 14 pt or higher. You want people to be able to see what is on your slide.

Even though most of the templates will go down to 12 pt, I figure if I'm getting that deep into subpoints, I can probably break the idea down better across a couple of slides.

Note that this rule goes out the window if it's a consulting-style presentation deck that is meant to be printed and handed out. In that case, I'd still recommend 8 pt or above and only use 8 pt for footnotes.

Font Size Consistency

Sometimes PowerPoint automatically adjusts the size of your text to make it visible in your text frame. For example, in the template I've been using for the screenshots for this book it took my text from 36 pt to 32 pt when I tried to have a title section with three lines in it.

Why should you care? Because it can be noticeable during a presentation if five slides are at 36 pt and then one slide is at 32 pt. Or if all of your bulleted points are at 18 pt and 16 pt and then suddenly there's a slide that's at 12 pt.

I will sometimes manually adjust my slides for that lowest common denominator (32 pt or 12 pt in the examples above) to keep the appearance consistent from slide to slide. (We'll cover that soon don't worry.)

Hierarchy of Elements

You want there to be a natural hierarchy among your elements. The font size of the title of a slide should be bigger than the main body text. And any subpoints should be the same or a smaller font size than the main points.

Also, at least in the U.S., the natural tendency is to start at the top and go downward and to start at the left corner and move towards the right. So top-left is usually where you should put whatever you want the audience to see first.

And when placing any other elements, like images or tables, etc. they should be below and or to the right of the text that introduces them.

Font Type

For most of the text in a presentation the goal is for it to be legible. Use workhorse fonts like Times New Roman, Garamond, Arial, etc. Also, if you're in a corporate setting know what the approved corporate font is and use that.

Summary Instead of Detail

When presenting to an audience you don't want to just stare at your slide and read it. You also don't want your audience to be so busy reading your slide that they don't listen to you.

Ideally, to avoid those problems, you will list one line per thought on a slide and then expand on that thought verbally. The text on a slide is more of a framework to work from, not everything you ever wanted to say about the topic.

Now, I will note that consulting presentation decks don't work this way. On those they seem to put every single thought they've ever had and then everyone sits around reading the slide instead of listening. It's almost like a written report in PowerPoint form. Consultants like them because they can still walk through the slides as if they're a presentation and rack up those nice billable hours. (Why, yes, I am jaded.)

Keep It Simple

Later we'll walk through animations and we're going to talk about how to change font colors, etc. But always keep the goal in mind, which is usually to convey information to your audience. If flying, spinning, whirring text helps you do that? Great, use it. If something like that will make your audience stop listening to you, then don't use it.

Same with colors and themes and everything else. Always ask yourself, "Does this help me get the message across?" If not, nix it.

Better to be boring and convey your message than have people talk about all the animations on your slides and forget what the presentation was about.

Contrast

There is a reason that black text on white backgrounds for generic products was so popular at one point in time. Because it works. Black on white, very legible. Very easy to see the words. Red on black? Not so much.

Red on green? Don't go there. Some people are red-green colorblind. Others are blue-yellow colorblind. That means they can't see the difference between certain colors, like blue and purple. So if you put blue text on a purple background, you maybe lose 8% of your audience right there.

Black text on a white background really is the best. Be creative in your headers and design elements, but make sure your main text is as legible as you can get it.

Make It Make Sense

We're not going to cover things like SmartArt in this introductory book, but when I do cover it in the intermediate book one of the things we will discuss is that you need to choose graphics that work for what you're trying to say. If you have connected arrows pointing to the right, your audience will expect that the first element on the left happens before or leads to the next element and so on and so forth. Don't use a graphic like that for unrelated points. Or list the points out of order. None of this:

You may brush your teeth before you eat breakfast, but you certainly don't do both of those before you wake up. Right? Always make sure your graphics in your presentation make sense.

* * *

Okay. Now let's discuss how to format your text.

Format Text Basics

There are four primary options for formatting text. With each you need to select your text before you try to use it.

The first is control shortcuts for common formatting like bold, italics, and underline.

The second, the one I use most often, is to go to the Font section of the Home tab and choose from the options listed there.

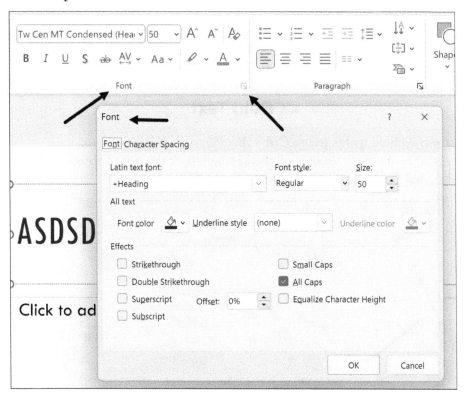

The third is to open the Font dialogue box. To do so, either click on the expansion arrow in the corner of the Font section of the Home tab (see the arrow pointing to the left in the image above) or right-click and choose Font from the dropdown menu.

Both options will open that dialogue box that you see above. Apply the formatting you want from there.

The fourth option is to use the mini formatting menu. If it doesn't appear when you select your text then right-click to bring it up along with a dropdown menu. Choose your formatting option from there.

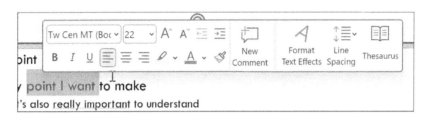

* * *

Now let's walk through all of your formatting options alphabetically. That will make this an easier section to refer back to later.

I am going to assume here that you have already selected the text you want to format, so I don't have to tell you to do that each time. Note that an easy way to select all of the text in a text box is to click into the text box and then use Ctrl + A.

Bold Text

The easiest way to bold text is to use Ctrl + B.

You can also in the Font section of the Home tab or the mini formatting menu, click on the bolded capital B in the second row of options:

Or in the Font dialogue box you can change the Font Style dropdown to either Bold or Bold Italic, depending on which one you want.

To remove bolding from text, you do the same thing. Select the text and then use Ctrl + B, click on the B in the menu, or change the Font Style in the Font dialogue box to Regular.

If you have text that is both bolded and not bolded and use either Ctrl + B or the B in one of the menu options, you may have to use it twice to get the result you want. It will take all of the text in one direction—bolded or not bolded—and if you were trying to go in the other direction, then you have to use Ctrl + B or the B in the menu one more time. The Font dialogue box does not have this same issue since you're specifically telling Excel which formatting you want to apply.

Font

Fonts are what dictate how your text looks. In the paste examples above, we saw the difference between a serifed font (Garamond) and a sans-serif font (Trebuchet MS).

When choosing a font, keep in mind readability. There are some nice, tried and true fonts that are used often for written documents because they work. Garamond and Trebuchet are two of them. Times New Roman and Palatino are a couple others.

If you work for a company, they may have a corporate font that they've designated for all of their communications. If that's the case, use that one.

You can either change your font before you start typing, or select all of your text afterwards and change it then.

Both the mini formatting menu and Font section of the Home tab have a dropdown menu for font where each font's name is written in that particular font so you can see what type of font it is:

By default, your font list is probably going to look like the list above. Those little clouds with arrows in them mean that if you want to use that particular font you need to download it from Microsoft.

(You can turn this off if you want so that only available fonts are shown. To do so, go to File, then choose Account in the bottom left corner, and click on Manage Settings under Account Privacy. Scroll down to the Connected Experiences section and uncheck the box for Turn On Experiences That Download Online Content. Another option is to uncheck the box that's a little further down that says Turn On All Connected Experiences.)

Back to the font listing.

At the top you'll see any fonts that are used by the theme in your current presentation. Below that you'll see any recently-used fonts. And then after that you'll see an alphabetical listing of all available fonts.

Usually, I'm trying to use a specific font. In that case, click into the field with the current font name and start typing. As you type the font name, Microsoft will autopopulate the name for you. When it lists the font you want, you're good, just click away.

For example, I just clicked into that field and typed "Ti" and it changed the value to Times New Roman for me. All I had to do was click away and my selected text updated to the new font.

If you're not quite sure of the font you want, but know the basic name, you can start with the dropdown menu open and then start typing the font name you want in that field. The dropdown menu will jump to that part of the alphabet and you'll be able to see all choices in that range and click on the one you want from the list.

I will note that PowerPoint was a little weird for me just now when I tried to type in a font name I didn't have. When I clicked away into the presentation, PowerPoint brought up a dialogue box where it tried to name the current font what I had just typed. If that happens to you, click on the No option and it will go away.

You can also use the Font dialogue box to choose a font. Use the Latin Text Font dropdown menu to do so. You won't be able to see the difference between the options there though, and I don't think it gives any additional functionality, so I never use it.

Font Change Case

To change the capitalization of a text selection, you can use the Change Case option available in the Font section of the Home tab. It's the option in the bottom row with an Aa and a dropdown arrow.

Your choices are Sentence Case, Lowercase, Uppercase, Capitalize Each Word, and Toggle Case. You can see in the screenshot below an example of each one applied to the text "this is sample text. and one more sentence. Last one."

Sentence case capitalizes the first letter in the first word of each sentence. Uppercase puts everything in all caps. Lowercase puts everything into lowercase. Capitalize Each Word changes the first letter of each word to a capital letter. Toggle Case flips the capitalization for every single letter.

For the lowercase and Toggle Case examples, the changes in the above image are subtle. For lowercase, you have to look at the L in the last sentence which is no longer capitalized. And for Toggle Case you have to realize that everything was capitalized except for that last L which was put into lowercase.

In the mini formatting menu, Change Case is not always going to be one of the available choices.

The Font dialogue box only gives you All Caps, which is the equivalent of Uppercase. It does also have Small Caps as an option, though, which I sometimes use in tables of contents or header sections.

Font Color

Both the Font section of the Home tab and the mini formatting menu have an A with a red line (at least initially) under it that allows you to change the color of your text. Click on the arrow next to the A to see sixty possible colors to choose from:

If you see a color you like, click on it to apply it.

In the generic presentation template your color choices are going to be the standard color choices you see in Word or Excel. There are shades of black and gray as well as columns for shades of blue, orange, yellow, and green along with a set of ten Standard Colors that are basically bright rainbow colors.

But here is that same dropdown when I'm in a presentation that has an assigned color scheme:

In this case, the Standard Colors and the first three black and gray columns of choices are the same, but then the other seven columns of color choices tie to the colors used in the theme. Which means if you choose one of those colors it's liable to work well with the other colors in the presentation. (Sorry if you're reading in print, you won't see that, but you can try it for yourself in PowerPoint.)

Sometimes, of course, you will need to use a specific color. For example, I have worked for employers who had assigned colors for their brand and all communications had to use very specific shades of each color.

In that instance, click on the More Colors option to bring up the Colors dialogue box. It has a Standard tab and a Custom tab, which look like this:

Click over to the Custom tab if you have RGB, HSL, or Hex code values for the color you need to use. Enter the relevant numbers, click on OK, and there you go.

The Font Color dropdown has one more option, the Eyedropper. Click on that option if you have an image or something else in your PowerPoint that uses the color you want. Your cursor will turn into an eyedropper when you do that.

You can either hold the cursor over your selection and it will show you the RGB values for that color, or you can click directly on the color you want to use and it will place that color in the Recent Colors section of the Color dropdown menu. Once you've grabbed the color or the value, it works the same as any other color.

The Font dialogue box also has the same color options but no Eyedropper.

Font Size

To change the font size, I usually go to the Font section of the Home tab, click on the dropdown arrow next to the current size, and select a new value:

Or I click into that box with the current font size and type the value I want if it isn't listed in the dropdown.

(If you ever select a range of text where the text is of varying sizes, the size you'll see in that font size field will show as X+ where X is the smallest font size in the selected range. So, 12+ for example where the size of the selected text ranges from 12 pt to 20 pt.)

Another option that I never use, but that you may want to use, are the increase font size and decrease font size options that are located to the right of the font size dropdown menu.

There's a bigger capital A with an up arrow and a smaller capital A with a down arrow. Click on either of those to change the font size one step up or down, respectively. The dropdown menu lists the font sizes that are used. So a 12 pt font will go up to 14 pt or down to 11 pt, for example.

These same options are also available in the mini formatting menu.

The Font dialogue box has a Size field. Click into the field and type in a new value or use the up and down arrows to change the font size by .1 pt at a time.

Italicize Text

The easiest way to italicize text is to use Ctrl + I.

In the Font section of the Home tab or the mini formatting menu, you can also click on the slanted I in the bottom row. It's between the options for bold and underline.

In the Font dialogue box, change the Font Style to either Italic or Bold Italic.

To remove italics from text, you do the same thing. Select the text and then use Ctrl + I, click on the slanted I in the menu, or change the Font Style in the Font dialogue box to Regular.

Keep in mind that if your text is mixed italics and regular text and you use an option other than the Font dialogue box, you may need to use the option twice.

Text Direction

By default the text in your presentation is going to be horizontal left-to-right. But there are other options available for text direction, namely rotated 90 degrees, rotated 270 degrees, and stacked. You can find this setting in the top right of the Paragraph section of the Home tab. The dropdown menu there lets you choose which option you want:

For text boxes, all of the text box has to share the same direction. So if you want different text to use different directions on the same slide, you need to use separate text boxes for each one.

Next to each option you can see a sample. So Rotate All Text 90 degrees turns the text so it runs downward and you'd have to tilt your head to the right to read it. Rotate All Text 270 degrees rotates it in the other direction so you have to tilt your head to the left. Stacked puts one letter per line but doesn't change how the letters are angled.

Clicking on More Options will open the Format Shape task pane on the right-hand side of your workspace, but the Text Direction dropdown menu there has the same four choices.

You may still want to use it though because it does give you a few other choices, including whether or not to Autofit your text to the text box, whether or not to shrink the text if it overflows the text box, and whether to resize the text box to fit the text.

This is also where you can say whether the text should wrap to a new line when it hits the edge of the text box.

Underline Text

For a basic, single-line underline the easiest choice is Ctrl + U. You can also click on the underlined U in the second row of the Font section of the Home tab or the mini formatting menu.

If you want more underline options than that, you need to use the Font dialogue box. As of now (late October 2023), there are sixteen underline options available there in the Underline Style dropdown:

You not only have a double underline choice, but also various dotted, dashed, and wavy line choices. Make your choice and then click OK to close the dialogue box and apply the change.

To remove an underline, you do the same thing again. For Ctrl + U and the U option in the menus, it will either remove a basic underline or transform a non-basic underline to a basic underline. Which means if you used a non-basic underline and try to remove it, you may have to use Ctrl + U or the U in the menus twice to do so.

For the Font dialogue box you just choose the none option from the dropdown menu.

As with italics and bolded text, if the text you select is both underlined and not underlined, you may have to use the Ctrl + U or the U option in the menus two times to get the result you want.

* * *

Clear Formatting

One final note. If you are working in a presentation that uses a theme—so has standardized fonts, colors, etc.—and you change your text away from that, but then later decide you want to go back to the standard look for that presentation, you can use the Clear All Formatting option in the top right corner of the Font section of the Home tab to do that.

* * *

Finally, if you look at the Font section of the Home tab you'll see that there are a few other formatting choices listed there such as strikethrough, character spacing, and text shadow. We're not going to cover them in detail in this beginner book, but they work the same. Select your text, click on the option you want to use, and done.

Format Paragraphs

The last chapter covered the basics of formatting individual letters or words. But sometimes the changes you need to make are at a higher level, the paragraph level or above. So that's what this chapter is for.

As with formatting text, my go-to is the Home tab. There is a Paragraph section there that has all of the options we're going to discuss here and a few more.

Sometimes an option may also be available in the mini formatting menu, but not all of them and not as consistently as with the font options.

You can also right-click in your workspace and choose Paragraph, Bullets, or Numbering from the dropdown menu, as needed. Paragraph brings up a Paragraph dialogue box while Bullets and Numbering both have secondary dropdown menus that let you choose the bullets or numbering to use.

One difference between text formatting and paragraph-level formatting is that you don't have to highlight all of the text to make a change if you're formatting a single paragraph. Just click somewhere in the paragraph and then apply the change you want.

Okay. Let's dive in and walk through some of these options.

Bulleted Lists

Many of the themes in PowerPoint come with bulleted lists already set up. So you bring up a Title and Content slide and you can see immediately that when you add text it will be bulleted. Like here with the Ion Boardroom theme:

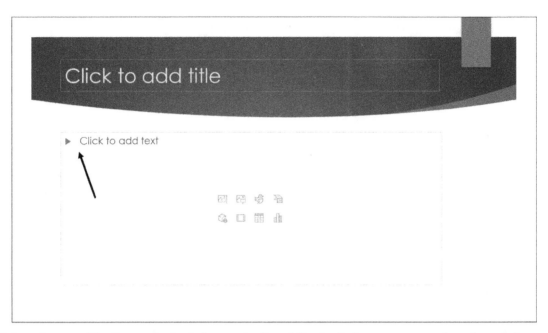

Other themes, like Integral, don't have a bulleted list built in or use one that doesn't have a visible marker. So if you want a visible marker for those themes you have to add it yourself.

To do this, option one is to add the bullet before you start. Click into that text box on your slide, go to the Paragraph section of the Home tab, and click on the dropdown arrow for Bullets:

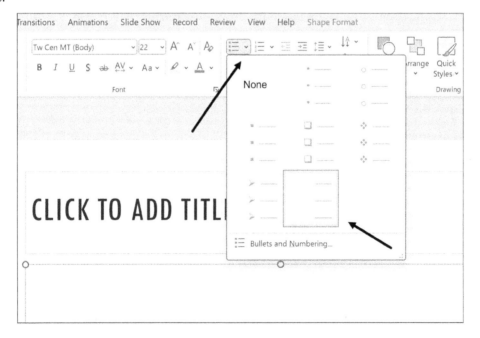

As you can see in the image above, this theme is using a bullet style that doesn't have a shape to it, so to a viewer it's as if there isn't a bullet. To change that, click on one of the six choices you can see there that do use a bullet. If you want there to be no bulleted formatting at all, click on None.

Once you do that, you'll see a grayed-out version of the bullet type you chose and when you start to type it will appear as a fully-colored bullet on the slide.

Here you can see one line of text that I already typed with the bullet fully visible. But since I haven't started typing on the second line that second bullet is grayed out:

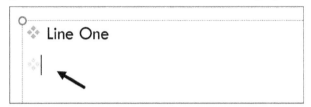

When you choose the type of bullet before you start typing, PowerPoint automatically defaults to creating a bulleted list for you. Each time you hit Enter, it will put a bullet at the start of the next line. If you don't want that, use the Backspace key to get rid of it.

Option two is to wait until you're done. Enter however many lines of text, select them all, and then choose your bullet type. PowerPoint will insert your chosen bullet at the left-hand side of each new line of text you entered.

Above I applied bullets by using the Paragraph section of the Home tab, but as I mentioned earlier, you can also right-click and use the secondary dropdown menu under Bullets:

If you click on the Bullets and Numbering option under that dropdown, it will open the Bullets and Numbering dialogue box, which lets you also control the size and color of the bullet:

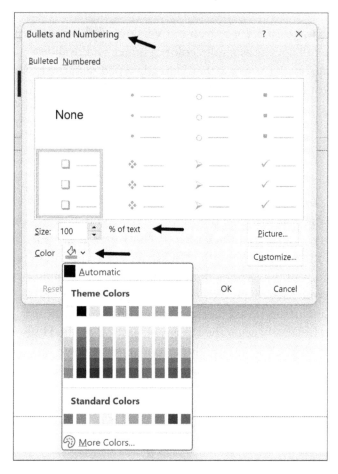

For most bulleted lists, when you hit Enter and then use Tab that will indent the next line of text and use a different bullet either in terms of size or type. You can change from that default, but if you do you may end up having a lot of manual formatting to do each time you want an indented bullet point.

(I'm assuming here that you will not try working with a master slide to make that change.)

This is probably easiest understood if we look at an example:

> ☐Default 1
>> ☐ Default
>>> ☐Default
>
> ☐Default 2
>> ○ Changed Bullet
>> ○ Carried Through Change
>>> ○ Carried through change
>
> ○ Carried through change

The first three lines here are what the default looks like if I use the shaded box bullet. Each time I indent, the bullet style stays the same, but it gets smaller.

The next four lines I made a change to the first subpoint. I changed the bullet used there to a circle. That then carried through to the next line and also to the subpoint after that next line. Which, all good.

But then…When I tried to create a new main point there at the bottom, it continued to use the circle shape.

So now that final line doesn't match the bullet point used on the other two main points. To fix that, I'd have to manually change it back. And then if I had a subpoint under that, I'd have to change that one to use the circle again.

Honestly, for me, not worth the headache. I'd just stick with the defaults. But there are people I have worked for that tend not to be the ones that do this work who do have strong opinions on what they want to see. So if you work for one of those, you may have to do some manual fixes to get the appearance they want.

If your slide is already using one type of bulleted list and you want to change all of the text on the slide to a different bulleted list, or like mine above to just standardize it to one list, click into the text box, Select All (Ctrl + A), and then make your choice in the Bullets dropdown.

Numbered Lists

Another option you have for points in a slide is to number them. I used to work for an employer who liked to use the Harvard Outline Format, for example. (Complete pain to work with—the format—and more money wasted on something insignificant than you can imagine. Consulting does not believe in the KISS principle.)

Alright. So. To create a numbered list, it works much the same way that a bulleted list does, except you want the Numbering dropdown menu:

I don't recall this being the case before, but maybe it was. Right now in PowerPoint as I try to create a multi-level numbered list, it just repeats the numbering choice on the next level. Like so:

I.   Point 1
   I.   Subpoint 1
   II.   Subpoint 2
      I.   Subsubpoint 1
      II.   Subsubpoint 2
II.   Point 2

See how I'm using a Roman numeral for the first level? And then it uses a Roman numeral for the second level? And the third? If I want to use some sort of standard outline format, that means a lot of manual edits. Because I will want Roman numeral followed by capital letter followed by standard number followed by lower case letter. And that is not what is happening here.

Good news is I can click onto any of the lines for a certain level under a point and change the numbering choice and it changes the associated lines as well. So it took two clicks and two changes to get this:

```
I.     Point 1
       A.    Subpoint 1
       B.    Subpoint 2
              1.     Subsubpoint 1
              2.     Subsubpoint 2
II.    Point 2
```

Now, it's possible you could set up a custom multi-level list in a Master Slide, but that's beyond us. I don't recommend mucking around in Master Slides unless you really know what you're doing because you can really screw things up.

For example, I started working at a new employer a couple months ago and I had to do a presentation, so I grabbed the corporate template we were supposed to use. And someone had borked the thing. You could not get a bulleted list to work at all if it had more than one level. Because someone who didn't know how to work in Master Slides had gone in there and accidentally limited the slide to only one level of bulleted points.

So this is the workaround I'm going to give you instead: If you have to do a multi-level numbered list for a PowerPoint slide, build it in Word. And then copy and paste that list into PowerPoint. It will keep the numbering formats you used in the other program and let you add more lines at each level without an issue.

One final note on numbered lists. Sometimes you will want to start on a number other than 1 or a letter other than A. To make that happen, click into the line you need to change, and then open the Bullets and Numbering dialogue box. (Using either the Numbering secondary dropdown menu when you right-click on the text, or the Numbering dropdown menu in the Paragraph section of the Home tab. Choose Bullets and Numbering from the bottom of either list.)

On the right-hand bottom side of that dialogue box it will say Start At and show a number in a box. Just change the number to what you need it to be. If you're working with letters, then A is equivalent to 1, B is equivalent to 2, etc.

Decrease List Level/Increase List Level

We've already covered one of your options for changing the list level of a point or numbered item. Tab indents or increases the item one level, Shift + Tab decreases it by one level.

But you also have options for this in the Paragraph section of the Home tab. In the top row are options for Decrease List Level and Increase List Level. So if you ever forget Tab and

Shift + Tab, you can always use those instead. They are located directly to the right of the bullets and numbering dropdown choices.

The left-hand one that points to the left is the Decrease List Level option. The right-hand one that points to the right is the Increase List Level option. Just click on your row and use the one you need.

These options are also part of the mini formatting menu.

Specify Amount of Indent

Sometimes you will need to have your text indented by a very specific amount and you won't be able to just use the default formatting in your PowerPoint theme. When that happens, right-click on a line that is at the level you need to fix, and choose Paragraph from the dropdown menu.

This will bring up the Paragraph dialogue box which lets you control Indents and Spacing: You can then change the Before Text value to indent your text the proper amount. Be careful,

because your changes will only apply to your selected text. Good news is it will carry through to new lines that you add from that point forward for that level. But if you wait to fix this until the end you may have a lot of fixing to do. (Or a lot of format painting to do, which we're about to cover.)

You can also use this setting with a standard paragraph of text that isn't bulleted or numbered if you want the text to sit away from the left-hand edge of your text box.

Format Painter

Sometimes you can save yourself a lot of effort by getting one line or paragraph formatted correctly and then using the Format Painter which is located in the Clipboard section of the Home tab and looks like a paintbrush.

What the Format Painter does is it takes the text color, font, font size, numbering style, bolding, italics, etc. from the text you select, and then applies that formatting to the text you tell PowerPoint to apply it to.

So in our messy bulleted and numbered list examples above, if I get the formatting on one subpoint the way I want it, I can select that text, click on the Format Painter, and then select the next line of text and it will transfer over all of my formatting for me.

At least for numbered or bulleted lists, right now it looks like I can just click into the line that has my formatting I want, click on the Format Painter, and then click on my other line and all of the formatting transfers. I don't have to select the entire line of text.

But if that doesn't work, then you may need to select the whole line of text or paragraph that's formatted the way you want before you use the Format Painter. Sometimes there's a little trial and error involved.

If you have multiple locations where you want to transfer formatting, you can double-click on the Format Painter when you select it. That will keep it turned on until you either click on it again or use Esc to turn it off.

A few cautions about the format painter.

It is a wonderful tool that can save you a lot of effort, but it will apply the formatting to the next text you click on. So be very careful where you click after you turn it on. If you mess up, use Ctrl + Z to Undo, and try again.

Also, at least in Word and I assume in PowerPoint too, sometimes the way you select the text will impact what formatting is applied. I've had situations in the past where I selected a paragraph starting at the top down and the Format Painter didn't capture the formatting I needed. But if I selected that same paragraph starting at the bottom, it did. So if it doesn't work the way you thought, try selecting the sample text in a different way.

If you need the formatting between paragraphs or bullet points to copy over, be sure to select multiple paragraphs or bullet points in your sample.

Also, know that the Format Painter takes *all* the formatting and transfers it, so be careful there. Sometimes it transfers a little more than you want it to transfer.

The Format Painter tool is also available from the mini formatting menu.

Text Alignment

The next significant formatting change that you may want to make at the paragraph level is the alignment of your text. So far we've been looking primarily at examples that are left-aligned with a ragged right-hand margin.

But you can center text, align it to the right, or justify it. This is best understood with a visual example:

This is a paragraph of text that has to cover multiple lines so we can discuss the difference between the different alignment options. This one is **left-aligned.**

This is a paragraph of text that has to cover multiple lines so we can discuss the difference between the different alignment options. This one is **centered.**

This is a paragraph of text that has to cover multiple lines so we can discuss the difference between the different alignment options. This one is right-aligned.

This is a paragraph of text that has to cover multiple lines so we can discuss the difference between the different alignment options. This one is **justified.**

The first paragraph there is left-aligned. That means that all of the rows of text along the left-hand side of the page are aligned. You can draw a straight line and connect the start of "this", "we", and "options". But note that the right-hand side is not aligned that same way. That's a ragged right-hand margin.

The second paragraph there is centered. Each line is equally distributed around an invisible center line that runs through that space. You can especially see that in the third line of text where there is a lot of space to the left and right of the text in that line.

The third paragraph is right-aligned. In this case, the words on each line all line up on the right-hand side ("so", "alignment", and "aligned") but the left-hand side is uneven or ragged. See how the second line is longer than the first and definitely longer than the third.

The final paragraph is justified. Both the left and right-hand sides are aligned. To make that happen, PowerPoint adds extra space between the words in the line. Usually the difference is so subtle no one notices, but if you use a lot of big words it can become very obvious. With justified the final line is simply left-aligned.

You can choose your text alignment options in the Paragraph section of the Home tab in the bottom row:

Each option is formatted like the choice. So here we have Align Left, Center, Align Right, and Justify. I have my cursor over the Center option in the screenshot above so that you can also see that each option has a control shortcut.

Ctrl + L will left-align, Ctrl + E will center, Ctrl + R will right-align, and Ctrl + J will justify your selected text. (The only one of those I use often enough to have memorized is Ctrl + E to center.)

The left, center, and right-align options are available in the mini formatting menu on the left side on the bottom. The justify option is on the right-hand side and may not always be available.

You can also choose your paragraph alignment option in the Paragraph dialogue box. It has one final option that isn't available elsewhere, Distributed. That is usually not something you'll want. It takes your text and forces it to cover the entire space in the text box even if that means placing large amounts of space between each letter. (This can be helpful for graphic design projects, but if you're creating book covers or something like that in PowerPoint there are far better tools for that out there.)

The text alignment options we just discussed are related to how the text is arranged left to right within a text box, but there are also options for how text is arranged in a text box top to bottom. Again, this is probably best understood with an image:

This is top-aligned text.		
	This is middle-aligned text.	
		This is bottom-aligned text.

On the left-hand side is the default option you'll normally see, top-alignment. The text starts in the top of the text box and as you add more text it will fill in the text box until it reaches the bottom.

The second example there is an example of middle-aligned text. In that instance, whatever text you add into the text box will be placed so that there is an equal amount of space in the text box above and below the text. As you add more text, your text will expand both upward and downward until you fill the text box.

The final example is bottom-aligned text which starts at the bottom of the text box and then fills the text box from the bottom to the top.

Here I've added another paragraph to each one so you can see the difference in how they handle additional text:

This is top-aligned text. I just added more text here.	This is middle-aligned text. I just added more text here.	This is bottom-aligned text. I just added more text here.

To apply this kind of alignment, click into the text frame, and then go to the Paragraph Section of the Home tab and choose the option you want from the dropdown menu.

The option for this one is a bit buried, at least for me. If you use a bigger screen it might not be as buried for you, but for me it's a tiny little icon on the right-hand side of the Paragraph section of the Home tab. It looks like a box with a line in the middle and arrows pointing up and down. But I can see that it's the one I want because if I hold my cursor over it it says "Align Text". Here it is:

Click on More Options to bring up a Format Shape task pane on the right-hand side of your workspace where you can use the Vertical Alignment dropdown menu to choose Top, Middle, Bottom, Top Centered, Middle Centered, or Bottom Centered. Those last three options combine the Center option with Top, Middle or Bottom.

By default this is not an option available in the mini formatting menu. (That menu is dynamic so if you recently used it then the option may appear for you to select, but since it's not guaranteed to be there, I just skip right past it and go to the Home tab.)

Columns

In the example above I had three separate text boxes to display that text. But if the effect you want is to have your text appear on the page in multiple columns like in a magazine layout, then the best way to do that is to use the columns option with a single text box.

Add your text or click into that text box, and then go to the Paragraph section of the Home tab. The Add or Remove Columns option is in the bottom row and by default shows two sets of lines side-by side:

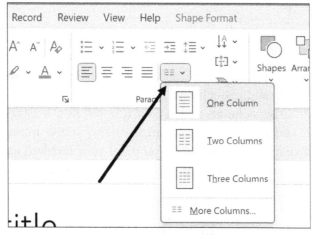

Click on the dropdown arrow and then click on the number of columns you want. If you click on the More Columns option at the bottom, that will open the Columns dialogue box where you can choose any number of columns you want as well as set the spacing between the columns.

Here is an example of the three columns option when I only have enough text for a column and a half:

This is text that I'm adding to this presentation so that we have enough text to see how multiple columns work in a text box.

plenty of text to work with.

And maybe one more.

Okay, good enough.

Let's go ahead and add yet another paragraph here so that we have

---

It's not very pretty, but it is a good example of how this works. PowerPoint took the text box (the black outline you can see) and divided it up into three sections. It then put text in the first section until that section filled, at which point it started to put text into the second section. Since I didn't have enough text to fill that second section, the bottom of the second section and the third section remain empty.

PowerPoint does not have column breaks like Word, so you can't insert a break to force text into the next column. (At least as of now, their Help specifically states this and says to submit a request if you'd like to see that.) So the only way to balance out your text across columns right now is to use Enter to add enough lines to force your text into place. Not ideal.

The nice thing about using columns is that your text will flow between the columns. But, if your text is pretty static and you want more control over what text appears where, it's probably just as easy to insert three identical text boxes and paste your text into each separate box.

So if you need multiple columns I'd experiment and see which approach works the best for you.

Line Spacing

Another way you can format lines of text is by changing the spacing either between the lines within a paragraph or between different paragraphs of text. For this one, I usually just right-click and choose Paragraph to use the Paragraph dialogue box.

Here are two paragraphs of text. For the first one the spacing between the lines of text within the paragraph is set to .9 which is the default. For the second one it is set to 1.9 which you can see in the dialogue box:

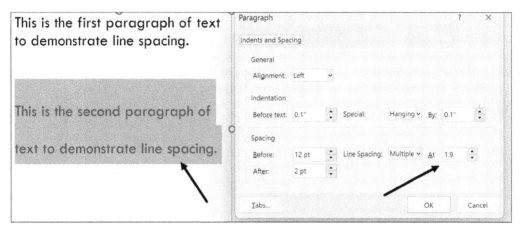

There is a significant difference there, right? That second set of lines don't even look like they belong together they're so far apart.

That Line Spacing dropdown has choices available for single, 1.5, double, exactly, and multiple line spacing. For exactly and multiple line spacing you can then add a value.

Now let's look at the spacing between two paragraphs. I've changed both paragraphs back to .9 spacing between the lines within the paragraph, but now I want to adjust the space between them.

To do that I either need to adjust the After value for the first paragraph or the Before value for the second paragraph.

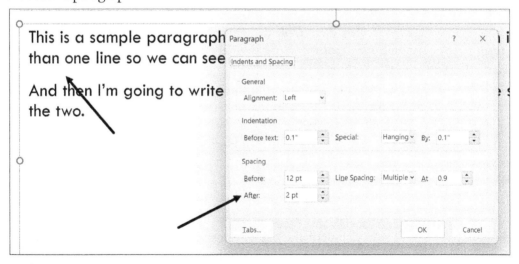

Here I've changed the Before value for the second paragraph to 12. You can see that there's about a line's worth of space between the two paragraphs when I do that.

If two paragraphs have different settings, so maybe one says 2 pt after and the other says 12 pt before and those overlap, PowerPoint combines the two values. So you get a 14 pt space.

Which means that sometimes if you're trying to fix spacing between two paragraphs you will have to look at the settings for both of them to figure out where that value is.

As I mentioned at the start of this section, I tend to right-click and choose Paragraph and go from there. But the mini formatting menu has a line spacing option that can appear on the right-hand side that lets you choose between 1.0, 1.5, 2.0, 2.5, and 3.0 line spacing.

The Line Spacing option is also in the top row of the Paragraph section of the Home tab:

If you click on Line Spacing Options at the bottom of either list it will open the Paragraph dialogue box.

Special Types of Indentation

One final item to discuss in that Paragraph dialogue box. In the Indentation section there is an option for Special with a dropdown menu that lets you choose between none, First Line, and Hanging and then lets you specify a value.

First line will take the first line of a paragraph and indent the text from the left side by a set amount but keep the rest of the lines in that paragraph aligned normally. You can see an example of that in almost all of the paragraphs in most print books. The first paragraph of a section or chapter usually doesn't do this, but every other paragraph usually does.

So if you need that for a paragraph, open the Paragraph dialogue box, choose First Line, and then set the value for indent.

Hanging does the exact opposite. It leaves the first line alone but then indents the rest of the lines of text. This is often used with a bulleted or numbered list where text wraps to the next line so that the text in each line of the paragraph starts at the same point. If you don't set the text to have a hanging indent then the second line of the paragraph will align with the bullet point or number instead.

* * *

Alright, so that's formatting text and paragraphs. A lot of basic beginner presentations just use text so that's where we're going to stop in this book. Because we still need to talk about how to give your presentation and all the fun little bits that go with that. If you want to use tables or charts or SmartArt or any of that, it's covered in the next book in this series.

Animations

If you've ever given a presentation, then you know the annoying feeling when you're trying to talk and your audience is scanning ahead on the current presentation slide rather than listening to you. That's where animations come in handy in PowerPoint. You can design the presentation so that each line of text or element on the slide appears separately.

Animation is added after the slide has been prepared, so enter all the text you want on that slide and then click onto the first line of text and go to the Animations tab:

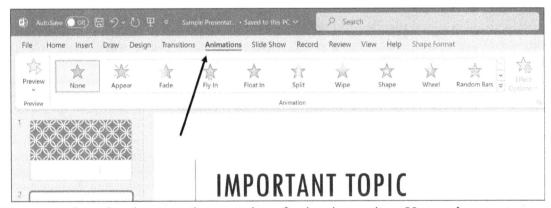

You can see here that there are a large number of animation options. You can have text appear, fade, fly in, float in, split, wipe, shape, etc., etc.

You do you, but I will tell you this from the perspective of someone who has given presentations to thousands of people at a time and also had to sit through hundreds of business presentations, that often the simplest approach (appear) is the best.

Remember, your presentation is there to support what you're trying to say, not to steal the show.

Just my opinion, but maybe ask yourself if this contributes to what you were trying to do or not when you're tempted to go a little overboard in terms of special effects.

Okay, lecture done.

Click on the type of animation you want to use from that Animation section of the Animations tab. PowerPoint will then add that type of animation to *all* of the bullet points in that slide that are at that level:

It will also number the items to show you the order in which they will appear.

So if you look at the image above, you can see that my first bullet point is numbered one but then the next two are numbered two. They're going to both appear at the same time unless I change that, because one is a subpoint so initially grouped with the main point. Finally, we have the third main bullet point which will appear third.

Most times I don't want the sub-point to appear at the same time as my main point. So I don't want the second and third line above to appear together. Which means I need to fix that. How do I do that?

First step is to click on the expansion arrow in the bottom of the Animation section of the Animations tab:

This will bring up the Appear dialogue box. Click over to the Text Animation tab:

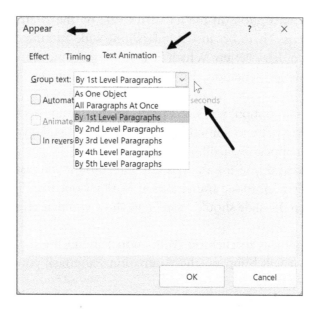

From there you can change the Group Text dropdown option. The default is By 1st Level Paragraphs which is why my subpoint is not set to appear separately.

In my presentation slide I only have two levels of points, so I could choose By 2nd Level Paragraphs and it would work just fine. But if I had a more complex slide then maybe I'd need to use By 5th Level Paragraphs to get each sub-subpoint to appear separately.

I made my choice and now you can see that each line of text will appear separately:

Perfect.

But I still want to see what I've set up. (Often this is crucial when there are photos or videos or other non-text elements on the slide.)

For me, the best way to test a slide like this is to just go to the Slide Show tab and start a presentation from that slide. (We'll cover that momentarily.)

Bring that up and then either left-click, use the down arrow, use the right arrow, or hit Enter when you want the next line to appear. Each of those options will show the next item or advance you to the next slide if there's nothing left. Esc to exit that preview.

There is also a Preview option on the left-hand side of the Animations tab, but it won't work with default settings. That's because it "plays" the slide and the default setting for these animations is to have no delay set up. Which is absolutely fine when you're up there clicking through and giving your presentation. But when you're trying to "play" the presentation, everything hits at once.

If you want to use that option, you need to go to the Timing section of the Animations tab and change the Delay value to something like 00:50. That will give enough of a delay for you to see each element appear by itself.

Keep in mind, too, that if you use the Appear animation it will just have the line show up on the slide. If you really want to see animations at work try one like Fly In or Float In. As you click on each new option the slide should "run" and show you that effect without you needing to Preview.

Another preview option is to click on Animation Pane in the top row of the Advanced Animation section. That will bring up the Animation Pane task pane that will also let you "play" your presentation.

Setting up bullet points like I did above is relatively easy to do. But sometimes I have different elements on my slides or I want the main points visible right away but not the subpoints. The way to create a more complex order is to use this Animation Pane.

As you can see above, it shows each of the animated items for that slide and the order in which they will appear. Each line also has symbols that are supposed to tell you what will make that line appear (a click by default which is represented by that white image of a computer mouse) and what type of animation will be used. Next to that you can see the text that starts that specific line.

It's better though to hold your cursor over each item to see a text description of what will happen. Because when I was just now experimenting with different animation styles on the same slide that little green star didn't change all that much:

And yet each of those first three lines there uses a different animation. You can see in the image above that I've held my mouse over that third line and it uses the Split animation style.

To do what I was just doing and apply different types of animation to different lines of text in your presentation (something that's probably not a good idea due to the distraction factor), just select each line individually and then click on the animation you want.

Okay, back to the Animation Pane.

When you click on a specific item in the Animation Pane, there's a dropdown arrow that appears at the very end of that line. Left-click on that arrow to choose a different way to start the line. Your options are click, with previous item, or after previous item by a set period of time.

Usually click is the option you want. But if you're going to have the slide run on its own for an audience, then the after previous item option would let that happen. Finally, with previous item will group two of your elements together so they appear at the same time.

For example, let's say you have two subpoints and you want both of those to appear together, but you don't want the third subpoint to appear just yet. You can't use the level setting we discussed before because it would apply the same rule to all three. But what you can do is go to the second of the two subpoints (assuming it's already set to appear after the first subpoint), and change the timing option for that second subpoint to Start With Previous. That should make both of those items appear at the same time.

To change the order in which an item appears, click on that line in the Animation Pane, and then use the up and down arrows at the top of the pane to move the item around in the numbered list. That will change the item number on the slide as well:

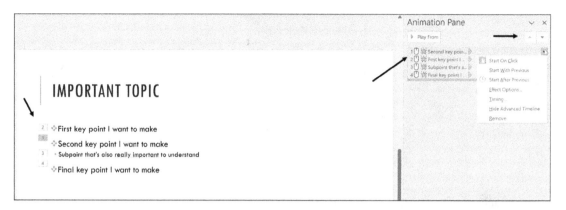

Here I moved that first line to the second appearance position and it is now numbered 2. If I run this slide, you will see "Second key point…" appear before "First key point…"

In the image above, the horizontal black arrow on the right-hand side is pointing to the up and down arrows you can use to shift an item up or down in the order.

You can also see the dropdown menu for that first row, which has the start options as well as timing and effect options. Those are also available in the Advanced Animation and Timing sections of the Animations tab.

If you expand your list of animation choices in the Animation section of the Animations tab, you'll see that there are also animation options for placing emphasis on an item in your presentation or for having an item exit your presentation. They work the exact same way.

As I said before, using animation is very handy sometimes. Just don't overdo.

Other Tips and Tricks

Before we move on to how to actually give a presentation, I wanted to touch on a few other tips or tricks that might be helpful.

Add Notes to a Slide

When I advised you to keep the text on your slides to the bare minimum, I can imagine that some of you thought to yourselves, "But then how do I remember that detail? Or what if I forget what the bullet point is about?"

Well, good news is that you can add notes to your presentation that are either, (a) visible when you print the presentation for yourself, or (b) visible on your computer as you present but not on the screen that participants see.

To add notes to your presentation slide, go to the right-hand side of the gray bar below your main workspace and click on Notes:

That will open a task bar at the very bottom of the screen that says "Click To Add Notes".

You can also go to the Show section of the View tab and click on the Notes option there to get the same task bar. However you manage to open it, simply click on that space and type in whatever note you want to add like I did here:

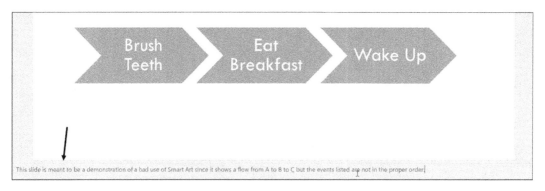

If you have a lot of text to add in the Notes section, you can make that section bigger by holding your mouse/cursor over the border between that notes pane and your slide until you see a white arrow pointing up and down. Left-click and drag upward. That will increase the size of the Notes section while decreasing the size of the slide.

We'll talk about printing later, but if you want to see how those notes look on a Notes Page printout, you can go to the Presentation Views section of the View tab and click on Notes Page. You'll see something like this:

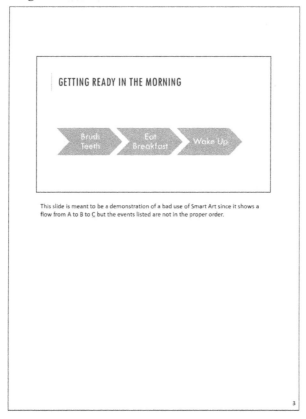

It has the slide at the top and then any added notes in the section below that. You can, if you want, print this for your participants, but remember that they will just read the notes instead of listen to you. So notes pages are best used for the presenter alone or as handouts after the fact.

To return to the standard view click on Normal in that Presentation Views section of the View tab.

Spellcheck

To run spellcheck on your presentation, go to the Proofing Section of the Review tab and click on Spelling. It should be the first option.

It works pretty much the same as in Word.

If there are no spelling errors, PowerPoint will just tell you that.

If there are spelling errors, PowerPoint will open a Spelling task pane on the right-hand side of the screen. That pane will identify the misspelled word at the top. Below that you can choose to Ignore Once, Ignore All, or Add (to the dictionary) if it's not a misspelling. If it is a misspelling, there will be a list of suggested words it could have been where you can click on one of the choices and then tell PowerPoint to Change this one instance or Change All to change all misspellings in the entire document.

If you're not sure which spelling is correct, below the suggestions box will be a definition for the currently selected option. (This can come in handy when trying to figure out whether you wanted discrete or discreet, for example.)

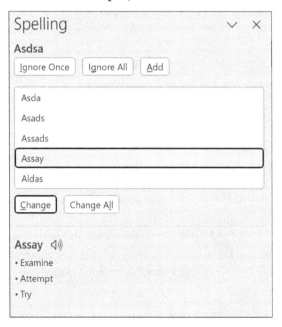

Do be careful with using Change All and Ignore All because they apply to all instances of that word and you don't get to evaluate each instance separately.

Also, just a reminder that spellcheck is not a substitute for a final readthrough. I will sometimes end up with a cuss word that I didn't mean to include because it's one letter off of the word I did mean to use. Spellcheck doesn't catch that.

It also doesn't work with similar words. Just now as I was proofing this document I had used "lest" instead of "lets". Spellcheck misses things like that. So you should read through one last time no matter what.

Find and Replace

Ctrl + F is the easiest way to find a word in your document. Using that will bring up the Find dialogue box where you can type the word you want. There are checkboxes below the field where you type what you're looking for where you can choose to match case and/or find whole words only.

So if I want to find all uses of "Tom", I'd check both of those boxes so I don't end up finding words like tomorrow as well.

Note that it does seem to also look in placeholder text that was used in a presentation. So, for example, I just searched for "to" in a presentation where I only had three slides and it brought up some slide masters that used phrases like "Click Icon To Add Picture."

If that ever happens to you and you need to get back to your presentation, go to the Slide Master tab and click on the Close Master View option.

Ctrl + H will bring up the Replace dialogue box which has fields for both what to find and what to replace it with. You also have options there for match case and find whole words only. Use them.

It can be especially important with replace to use those boxes because you don't want to accidentally turn "tomorrow" into "Steveorrow" when what you really meant to do was replace "Tom" with "Steve".

You can bring up both the Find and Replace options via the Editing section of the Home tab as well if you ever forget the control shortcuts.

Replace Font

The Editing section of the Home tab is the only place I know of where you can replace a font. Click on the dropdown arrow for Replace and you'll see an option there for Replace Fonts.

This will open the Replace Font dialogue box, which has a dropdown for which font you want to replace and which font you want to use instead. Make your choice and then click on Replace.

The dialogue box *does not* default to your current font so you need to know what fonts you're already using before you try this.

Also, it did not work on SmartArt for me just now, so you'll need to scan through your presentation and see if there was any text you thought should've changed but didn't.

And, finally, be careful with this if you have a lot of fancy formatting or lots of text in your presentation already, because sometimes fonts that are the same point size take up different amounts of space on the page. That means formatting that worked for your original font may not work for the replacement font and you'll need to fix that.

One more thing, it may not be perfect. I used this on a work presentation template someone had set up using a font that wasn't available. And it did replace that font in everything I can see on the slides, including the master slides. But, every single time I open that presentation it also tells me that the font I replaced is missing. So clearly somewhere it didn't get replaced, but I wasn't able to find it and neither was this replace font option.

Undo/Redo

We discussed this in the basic terminology section, but I wanted to circle back to the Undo option and also discuss Redo.

Undo will back out of what you just did. If I apply a font to text and don't like it, the easiest way to change that back is Ctrl + Z.

If you ever undo something and then change your mind and want it back, the easiest way to do that is Ctrl + Y.

But sometimes you may take multiple steps before you realize you want to undo something. For example, maybe I add a table to a presentation and I do a lot of fiddly little formatting to it where I change column widths, add text, and change colors and then at the end of the day I realize that, no, I just need to back out those last five or six steps.

In that case, the best option is the Undo arrow at the very top of the workspace. It's the arrow pointing to the left and will always be available as long as you've done something in the presentation. (If you've yet to do anything it will be grayed out.)

Click on the dropdown arrow on the right side of that Undo option, and you'll see a listing of the last X number of steps you took. Here we have sixteen steps that can be undone but the list can be longer than that:

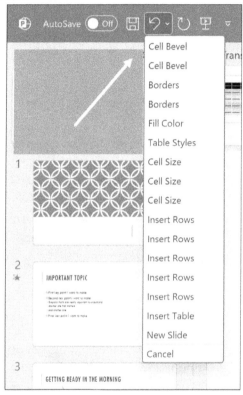

The top item is the last thing you did. The bottom item is the oldest step that you can undo.

Each item listed gives you some idea what it was about but not a great idea, so you kind of have to know what you just did or how far back you want to go.

In this case, if we look from the bottom up, I inserted a new slide, added a table, expanded that table from two rows to seven, and then started changing the column widths and messing around with formatting of the table.

If I want in one step to go back to that original inserted table without all that additional formatting, then I could click on the last of the listed "Insert Rows" entries in that list.

That undoes everything that happened after that point. I am now back to a new slide with a two-row table in it.

Now, maybe I messed that up. I undid all of that and now I have a table with only two rows and all of the columns are all the same width. But I actually wanted those five rows I'd added.

To Redo part of what I just undid, I can use Ctrl + Y or click on the arrow at the top that points to the right. Sadly, as I write this, I can only do so one step at a time. But it is pretty easy to use Ctrl + Y multiple times and I honestly rarely need to redo something I undid.

Zoom

You can zoom in or out on your presentation slides by using the slider in the bottom right corner of your workspace.

The bar perpendicular to the line shows where you currently are in terms of zoom level. The actual percentage is listed at the far right of the bar.

By default mine is zoomed to 97% for a new presentation, but that changes as additional task panes appear. When the Designer tab opens, it drops to 80%, for example.

To change the zoom level on your slide, either click on the bar to the left or right of the current marked spot or left-click on that marker and drag until the main workspace is the size you need.

You can also go to the Zoom section of the View tab and click on Zoom to bring up the Zoom dialogue box, which lets you choose from 400%, 200%, 100%, 66%, 50%, and 30%. You can also change the Zoom to Fit value to any percentage you want.

I often use this to get back to 100% when needed.

Note that with Zoom, the size of the slide changes but not the size of the workspace where the slide displays. So if you go for a high zoom percentage you will not see the full slide.

This is different from how the slide workspace will resize when you change the size of a taskpane that surrounds that workspace. So sometimes it may work better to click and drag along the edge of one of the visible task panes to make more space for the main slide area in your workspace.

Headers and Footers

If you want to print your presentation slides, chances are you may want to include headers or footers. To do so, go to the Insert tab and click on the Header & Footer option in the Text section. That will open the Header and Footer dialogue box:

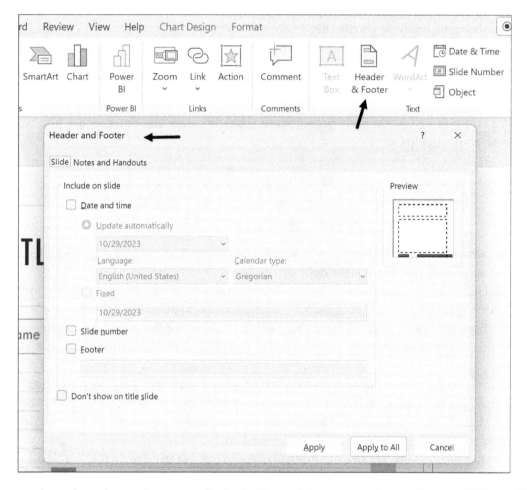

Your options for what to insert are limited. On a slide you can insert Date and Time, Slide Number, or a custom Footer.

You can also choose to not include that information on the title slide but just include it on every other slide in the presentation.

For Notes and Handouts, you can choose between Date and Time, Page Number, a Header, and a Footer.

As you click on each choice, the little thumbnail image on the right-hand side will put a black box where that element will appear. You can't change the location that element will appear in unless you go and change your master slides, which we are not going to do. So you're stuck with wherever that element is set up to appear for your chosen presentation theme.

Present Your Slides

Okay. You've created a presentation. Congrats. Now it's time to present it. How do you do that?

Go to the Start Slide Show section of the Slide Show tab, and click on From Beginning or From Current Slide on the left-hand side:

Usually you want to do From Beginning unless you're testing a presentation slide, in which case the option that lets you just start at the current slide is very handy.

If you're on a laptop or desktop computer and not connected to another monitor or anything like that, your entire screen should now be the presentation. You'll either start with the first slide or the last one you'd had selected, depending on the choice you made.

To navigate to your next slide or bring up any text on your current slide that was set to appear, you can left-click, use Enter, or try the right or down arrows.

If you ever go a little too far and want to go back a slide or a bullet point, use the up or left arrows.

You can also right-click and choose Next or Previous, but I never use that.

To exit your presentation before you're done, use Esc. Otherwise when you reach the end of the presentation the screen will be black and you'll see a message that says "End of Slide Show, Click to Exit." You can left-click or Esc will work there too.

There are some fancier options to choose from if you right-click on a presentation, like what your pointer looks like under Pointer Options, but if you're going to use them get those set up before you start presenting.

You can also see the Presenter View by right-clicking. So if you want to know what that view will look like while just working with your own screen, that's how to do that.

The Presenter View looks like this:

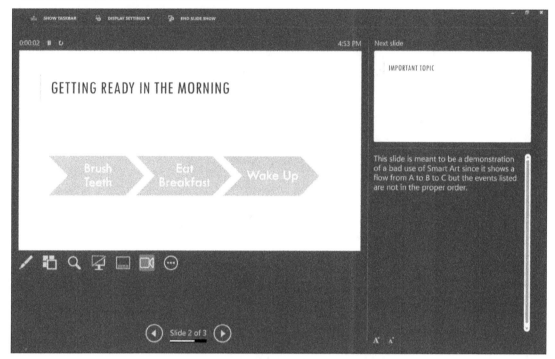

Your current slide is on the left-hand side. The notes related to that slide are on the right-hand side bottom section. Above the notes on the right-hand side, you can see which slide is up next and what it will look like when it appears.

So, for example, that next slide actually has four bullet points on it but in this preview we don't see them because when that slide comes up it will not show those automatically since I have them set to appear one at a time.

If you have your computer connected to an external monitor or a projector, Presenter View should launch automatically. The current slide will show on the external monitor or projector and your screen will show the next slide and notes.

There are some additional options below the current slide that you may want to play around with as well, but we won't cover here.

You can turn Presenter View off by right-clicking and choosing Hide Presenter View.

Print

Often it's a good idea in smaller group settings to also print your presentation slides so people can take notes as they listen to you.

You can find your print options by going to the File tab and then clicking on Print. Or use Ctrl + P. Both will bring up the Print screen:

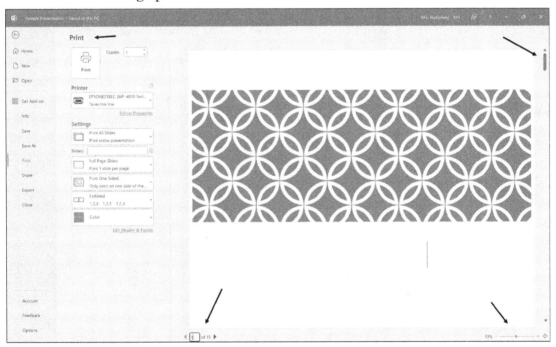

On the left-hand side in the second panel under the heading Print are your print options.

To the right of that is the preview section that takes up most of the space on the screen. That section will show you how the presentation will look when printed.

Below the preview are navigation arrows that let you move from page 1 to 2 to 3, etc. or back. There are also scrollbars on the right-hand side of the current visible slide that will let you see the other pages that are going to print. And in the bottom right corner is a slide where you can adjust the zoom level.

Now let's talk about all those settings under Print.

* * *

Print

At the very top of the print options is the button you click on to actually print. It's currently a square with a black and white icon of a printer that says Print below the icon.

Copies

Next to that is where you specify the number of copies to print. Click into the box and type the number you want or use the up and down arrows to change the value.

If you have never printed this presentation before, it might be a good idea to start with one copy and review it before you print twenty or a hundred or however many copies.

Printer

Directly below those options is a dropdown where you can select which printer to use.

Mine defaults to Microsoft Print to PDF because a few years back I noticed that if I had an Office program open and that program listed my personal printer as the default printer that it sometimes took a very long time for the program to open. So I always have to change this setting to my actual printer when I need to print.

I think the default setting is for Office to list your most recently used printer.

Printer Properties

Under the printer dropdown is a link for Printer Properties which will open a dialogue box with choices. You need to have your printer selected before you use this since the options available will be impacted by the printer you're using.

This is generally where you'd go to choose your paper or print tray if needed.

Settings

Under Settings you have a few choices to make. Make sure your printer is selected before you use this section.

Print All Slides / Print Selection /
Print Current Slide / Custom Range

The first choice is which slides to print. The default is Print All Slides. That will print all of your slides.

Print Selection requires that you already selected a subset of slides before you clicked on print. Print Current Slide will print the slide that was showing in the workspace when you chose to print.

Custom Range will take you to the Slides field directly below that dropdown. You can then enter which slide numbers to include. Commas between numbers means to print each one you list. So, 3,6,9 will print slides 3, 6, and 9. But a dash between numbers means to print the range. So, 3-9 will print slides 3, 4, 5, 6, 7, 8, and 9. You can combine commas and dashes so something like 3,4,5-7 will print slides 3, 4, 5, 6, and 7.

Click away from that box and the preview section will update to show the slides that will print.

If you have sections in your document, which we did not learn in this book, the section names will also be options for you to choose at the bottom of the dropdown menu. PowerPoint will print all of the slides in that one section if you choose one of the options listed there.

Slides

If you're trying to print a custom range, you can just skip using the dropdown altogether and go straight to the Slides field and put in the slides you want. PowerPoint will change the dropdown to Custom Range for you.

Print Layout and Handouts Dropdown

The next dropdown menu defaults to Full Page Slides so that's the title you'll see, but there are a lot more options under that if you click on the dropdown arrow.

With Full Page Slides each printed page will have one slide per page and it will fill the page.

The Notes Pages option will print with your slide on the top third of the page and any notes displayed under that. So this is a good one for you as the presenter, but maybe not for your audience because you want them to listen to you not read the slides.

The Outline option just prints the freestanding text on each of the slides in a long list. It will not print the contents of tables or any images or anything else.

The 1 Slide Handout option puts the slide in the middle third of the page with open space above and below it.

The other slide handout options with 2 to 9 slides per page do exactly what they say. They fit 2, 3, 4, 6, or 9 slides onto the page arranged either vertically or horizontally. You can see what each option will look like in the preview section.

Below all those choices there are also some options that you can check or uncheck by clicking on them.

They are: Print Slide Number On Handouts, Frame Slides, Scale to Fit Paper, High Quality, Print Comments, and Print Ink. Experiment with selecting or unselecting each one until you get the preview appearance that you want.

For example, my sample presentation had comments still in it. When I went to print, PowerPoint wanted to print an entire page for one of my slides that was just the comments for that slide. It also wanted to mark that slide as having a comment on it. I didn't want that, so I had to click on the Print Comments option to uncheck it.

Print One Sided /Print on Both Sides (Long) / Print on Both Sides (Short)

The next option lets you choose whether to print on one side of the page or on both sides of the page. This will only be visible if the printer you have connected to allows that. For slides or other landscape layouts (where the top is longer than the sides) you generally want to print on both sides and flip on the short edge. For notes pages or other layouts that are longer along the side than across the top you generally will want to flip on the long edge.

Collated / Uncollated

Here you choose whether to print one presentation at a time (collated) or each page of the presentation X number of times before printing the next page (uncollated). Which choice you want will depend on whether you want people to have the full presentation up-front or whether you intend to hand out each page of the presentation as you reach it.

Color / Grayscale / Pure Black and White

This option lets you choose whether to print in color, grayscale, or pure black and white. The black and white option strips out colored sections and makes them white not black, so it's the option that will use the least amount of ink. The grayscale option keeps those colored sections but transforms them to shades of gray. It's easy enough to see what each one will look like by making your choice in the dropdown menu and then looking in the preview section.

Edit Header & Footer

At the very bottom there is a link you can click on to edit the header and footer sections of your presentation. Click on that to bring up the Header and Footer dialogue box which we discussed earlier. Note that it has two tabs, one for Slides and one for Notes and Handouts, so you need to make your choices on the correct tab.

Page numbers are always good to have. I often like to also include the name of the presentation and author even if that's already on the title slide since slides can become separated.

Conclusion

Alright, that's pretty much it for a beginner-level introduction to PowerPoint. It's probably not everything you're going to need because we didn't cover inserting tables or images into your presentations. Nor did we cover SmartArt or WordArt. But I like to keep these books to a certain length that isn't too overwhelming and I think we've hit that point. So I'll cover the rest of that in the next book in the series.

If you don't want to continue on with me, you can, now that you have the basics, use PowerPoint's help options to get the rest of the way there.

In PowerPoint 365 as it exists in October 2023, Help can be found as a separate tab on the far right set of the tab choices. Click there and you'll see five options: Help, Contact Support, Feedback, Show Training, and What's New.

For users of 365, it's probably especially important to occasionally check in on that What's New option because 365 is constantly evolving, and sometimes the changes may be big ones or ones that would make your life easier if you knew about them. They certainly have been with Excel over the last couple years where some really great new functions have been added.

If you click on the What's New option it should open a task pane on the right-hand side of the workspace that has links to what they've added recently.

(Of course, nothing is ever perfect so when I was writing the first draft of this book that wasn't working for me at the time. The problem with all these connected options is that sometimes that connection fails and then you have nothing there.)

Anyway.

Help works the same way. You click on the Help option in the Help section of the Help tab and it opens a Help task pane where you can look up a topic that you want to learn more about:

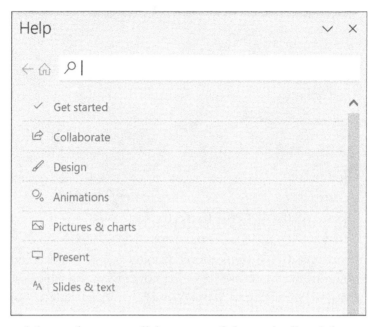

Either use the search bar at the top or click on one of the topics listed there to see more about that topic. There's text descriptions as well as videos.

You can also usually just hold your mouse or cursor over each of the options under a tab and PowerPoint will give you a description for that particular task. Like here where I held my mouse over the Shapes option:

Often those descriptions have a Tell Me More choice that you can click on to bring up Help specific to that option. That will once again open the Help task pane, but this time to that particular topic.

Now, what do you do when Office has put all of their help topics online and your version of PowerPoint seems to not be willing to connect to them like, oh, I don't know, me when I was writing the first draft of this section?

You can always do an internet search. I usually type "microsoft powerpoint 365" and then whatever topic I'm trying to learn about like "shapes".

Often the top result or one of the top results is from the Microsoft website. I look for links that say support.microsoft.com first or in this case the top link was microsoft.com. Those are the best place to start. Microsoft has really good help available, it's usually going to be up-to-date, and you don't risk clicking on something you shouldn't.

Google these days also has little answers to questions they pull onto their search results. Sometimes those work, too. They also tend to offer video links, which often are also good resources.

Personally, I tend to avoid watching random Office videos online because I once found a great helpful video on a topic that answered my question wonderfully only to realize that it was a complete rip-off of a video someone else had done a year before that.

Since I try not to reward assholes for being assholes that copy the hard work of others, that made me avoid random dude on the internet publishing tech help videos. But you do you. If you need the answer, you need the answer. I just always try to start with the official resource first.

Okay, so that's about it. Reach out if you have a question and can't find the answer. I don't check email every day these days, but I do check in and will try to help. And if you want to learn more from me then check out the next book in this series, *Intermediate PowerPoint 365* which covers tables, images, videos, SmartArt, and more.

Intermediate PowerPoint 365

POWERPOINT 365 ESSENTIALS - BOOK 2

M.L. HUMPHREY

CONTENTS

Introduction

In *PowerPoint 365 for Beginners* we covered the basics of working in PowerPoint, including how to choose a design theme to work with, how to add, edit, and format text, and how to present or print your presentation.

This book continues from there and explores intermediate-level topics like how to add tables, images, and charts to a presentation. It will also cover how to work with SmartArt and Shapes. We'll also touch on some more obscure topics such as inserting 3D Models and Equations or creating sections in your presentation.

Note that I am writing this in October 2023 and that Office 365 is a constantly evolving product. So most of what I say here should remain relevant long-term, but I can't guarantee that they won't change the program in some way that means what I tell you here no longer works quite the same way.

At the end of this book we'll touch again on how to find additional help if you ever need it. As long as you know that something is possible, even if they change things slightly, you should still be able to do it with a little boost from the help function.

Okay, then. Let's get started with a recap of the terminology I'm going to use in this book.

Basic Terminology Recap

These definitions were already covered in *PowerPoint 365 for Beginners*, so I'm going to go through them fast. Even if you think you know them all, at least skim if you haven't read the beginner book because I may have my own quirks and you'll need to know them to understand the rest of the book.

Tab

I refer to the menu options at the top of your PowerPoint workspace as tabs. This is because in older versions of Office when you selected an option at the top of the screen, it looked like a file tab. In more recent versions of Office they've eliminated that appearance so that now the selected tab is simply underlined.

Examples of tabs are Home, File, Insert, Draw, etc.

Click

If I tell you to click on something, that means to move your cursor over to that option and then use the mouse or trackpad to either left- or right-click. If I don't say which, left-click.

Left-Click / Right-Click

Left-click simply means to use the left-hand button on your mouse or to press down on the left-hand side of your track pad. (For me on my track pad, it's the bottom of the track pad, but I think some have those buttons at the top instead.)

Right-click simply means to use the right-hand button on your mouse or to press down on the right-hand side of your track pad.

Left-Click and Drag

If I ever tell you to left-click and drag this just means to go to that selection, left-click and hold down that left-click while moving your mouse or cursor until you've selected all of the text, images, etc. or until you've moved that object where it needs to go.

Select or Highlight

Before you can make changes to your text, such as size, font, color, etc. you need to select the text you want to edit. If I ever tell you to select text, that means to go to one end of that text, and then left-click and drag to the other end so that the text is highlighted.

Another way to select text is to click at one end of the text you want to select, hold down the Shift key, and then use the arrow keys to select the text you want. You can also select separate sections of text by selecting the first one and then holding down the Ctrl key as you left-click and drag to select the next section of text.

To select an object, left-click on it. When an object is selected, there will be circles around the perimeter of the object.

To select more than one object, you can click on the first one and then hold down the Ctrl key as you click on the next one.

Ctrl + A can be used to Select All. If you are clicked into a specific text box and you use it, you will select all of the text in that text box. If you are not clicked into a specific text box, then Ctrl + A will select all of the objects on the page.

Dropdown Menu

Often there will be additional choices available if you right-click somewhere in PowerPoint. I refer to this additional set of options as a dropdown menu even though sometimes it will actually drop upwards instead of downwards.

You can also find dropdown menus in the options at the top of the workspace under the tabs where there's an arrow to the right or bottom of an option.

Expansion Arrow

Another way to see more options in that top menu is to click on the expansion arrows that are sometimes visible in the bottom right corner of various sections. Clicking on an expansion arrow will either open a dialogue box or a task pane.

Dialogue Box

The old-school way for Office programs to show you additional options was to use dialogue boxes which appear on top of the workspace. Some of the expansion arrows will open a dialogue box as will some of the dropdown menu options. You can see one if you right-click in the main space and choose Font from the dropdown menu or if you click on the expansion arrow in the Font section of the Home tab.

To close a dialogue box, click on the X in the top right corner.

Task Pane

In newer versions of Office, they tend to use what I refer to as task panes. These are separate work spaces that are visible to the sides or sometimes below your main work area.

You can close a temporary task pane by clicking on the X in the top right corner. You can also left-click and drag to undock a task pane and move it around. Or you can change the task pane's width by holding your mouse over the inner margin until you see an arrow that points left and right and then left-clicking and dragging to your desired width.

Mini Formatting Menu

If you right-click in the main workspace you will see at the top or bottom of the dropdown menu a mini formatting menu with the most common formatting options. This can be especially useful when working on a computer with a small screen where the menu options up top are not fully visible.

Scrollbar

To navigate between slides in a large presentation and through a long list of options in a dropdown menu, you will need to use the scrollbars. They run along the right-hand side or bottom of a given space when needed.

Control Shortcut

A control shortcut is when you hold down the Ctrl key (or sometimes another key) and then the specified letter to perform an action. So if I write Ctrl + C, that means hold down the Ctrl key and the C at the same time to copy something.

Undo/Redo

Ctrl + Z will undo the last thing you did. Ctrl + Y will redo the last thing you undid.

There is also a dropdown menu at the very top of the page with a backward-pointing arrow that will let you undo multiple steps at a time.

Slider

Some options in PowerPoint use a slider, which is a horizontal bar with a perpendicular line along the bar that marks the percent value currently being used. You can click along the slider or drag that perpendicular line to change the value.

Add Other Items to a Presentation Slide

In *PowerPoint 365 for Beginners* we focused on how to do a basic presentation that only used text. Now we get to cover the many, myriad other options you can add to a standard presentation slide.

If you look at a blank presentation slide that's been set up for it, you will see that there is usually a "Click To Add Text" note at the top of the main text box, but then somewhere below that text is a faded grid of icons. Like this:

There are currently eight of these icons in my version of PowerPoint. They are, in order from top left and across and then bottom left and across, Stock Images, Pictures, Insert an Icon, Insert a SmartArt Graphic, Insert Cameo, Insert Video, Insert Table, and Insert Chart.

These icons may not stay the same and they may not stay in the same position. For example, in the two weeks since I wrote the first draft of this book and now when I'm editing it, they put Insert Cameo in there and removed Insert 3D Model. In the five years since I wrote the first PowerPoint guide, they've changed the order of these icons and increased the number from six to eight.

Good news is if you hold your mouse over each one it will tell you what it is.

Also, you can always use the options in the Insert tab to add any of these as well as a couple others:

Stock Image is under the Pictures dropdown menu and Video is at the far end of the Insert tab, but you can see all the rest in the screenshot above as well as a few other choices like Shapes.

I am going to devote an entire chapter each to Tables, Pictures, Videos, SmartArt, Shapes, and Charts. But before we cover those I want to very briefly touch on Stock Images, Icons, 3D Models, and Cameos.

Stock Images

Click on the icon for Stock Images in a text box or click on the dropdown menu for Pictures in the Images section of the Insert tab and then choose Stock Images from there. Either way will bring up the Stock Images dialogue box.

By default it shows you a series of random stock photos, but there is also a search box you can use that will let you search for stock images by topic.

I'm not including a screenshot of that here because using stock photos can sometimes be an issue if you don't have the correct rights to use them. In general, stock is supposed to be safe, but it's always a good idea to read the fine print when using someone else's images. That's also why I'm not covering this topic in detail.

If you're just using stock images for a personal, small group presentation that won't be posted online, you're probably fine to use stock images.

If you're going to use them as part of an online course you sell or as part of a for-pay conference or in a YouTube video or something like that, you need to be more careful. That's commercial use and there may be limits you need to respect. Better to pay for your own stock photos off of a site like Shutterstock or Depositphotos and know exactly what your license allows, because the fines for misuse of a stock photo can be pretty steep.

Also, in this day and age, be very careful with any image that could be AI-generated since that hasn't shaken itself out at this point and most AI models were trained without permission on the copyrighted work of other artists. It's a possibility you could either lose any copyright you have in what you created if you use AI art as part of it, or that there could be a finding of damages at some point for people who used AI art without compensating the artists.

(If you're on the other side of that argument and think AI is great, don't reach out to me about it. Not interested in that conversation. Go find some online forum to be an AI champion. I'm just putting that caution out there.)

Anyway. To use stock images, find the image you want, click on it, and click on Insert. PowerPoint will then insert the image into your presentation. From there it will work just like a picture you insert, so see that chapter for those details.

Icons

PowerPoint also has a large number of icons that you can insert into your presentation. Either click on that Icons option in the text box or go to the Illustrations section of the Insert tab and click on Icons from there.

Both options will bring the Stock Images dialogue box up but it will be set to the Icons tab. You'll see a series of choices displayed and there will also be categories you can click on along the top as well as a search box. Find the icon you want, click on it, and choose Insert.

An icon is essentially a simplified line drawing of an object. If you want it to be a color other than black, you can insert it into your document and then go to the Graphics Styles section of the Graphics Format tab that will appear when you're clicked on the icon, and change the Graphics Fill color using the dropdown menu there.

Icons insert at a standard size but you can resize them by clicking and dragging on one of the white circles at the corner when the object is selected. (Don't drag from the sides because it will resize disproportionately and look weird.)

To move that object, left-click and drag when your cursor looks like arrows pointing in four directions which will generally be when you're near the perimeter of the object or on top of the illustrated portion.

3D Models

To insert a 3D model into your presentation slide, go to the Illustrations section of the Insert tab and click on the dropdown under 3D Models. This Device will let you find a 3D model you have saved on your computer. Stock 3D Models will let you use one of the Microsoft-provided models.

My cautions about using stock images apply to 3D models as well.

When you click on the 3D Models option for stock, you will see a dialogue box labeled Online 3D Models that has a series of categories to choose from as well as a search box. Mine right now is showing animated models, animated animals, animated for education, emoji, chemistry, anatomy, clothing, furniture, etc.

Click on the category and then select the model you want to insert and choose Insert.

I currently have an animated dog wagging its tail on my presentation slide. If you choose an animated option, you can click on pause in the bottom left corner of the text box that contains the 3D model to stop it from moving. Click on play to start it back up.

When the model is selected in your presentation there will be a circle with rotating lines up and down and then around in a circle that sort of reminds me of one of those atom drawings I saw back in chemistry class, but this one just has two sets of lines.

You can left-click on that and drag to rotate your 3D image.

For me, with the dog I chose, that's a little weird when I move it up or down. But side-to-side works well. With enough clicks and drags I now have a dog facing away from me and wagging its little tail at me.

These models are one of those things that can either be really useful or really distracting.

Cameos

Cameos are new for me, but since they chose to replace 3D Models with Cameos in that little list of choices, I feel I have to cover it to some extent. But if what I say doesn't make sense, then ignore it.

When I hold my mouse over Cameo in the Camera section of the Insert tab it tells me this is to "add your camera feed directly into your slides." You can choose to do this for this one slide or all slides from that dropdown. The icon that you can click on seems to match up to the one slide option.

Click on either the one slide option in the Insert tab or on the icon in your text box and it will fill that text box with an image of a stylized smiling person and open the Camera Format tab. By default, Preview is turned off. If you click on Preview in the left-hand side of that tab, you'll see whatever your computer camera shows.

So, if I'm understanding this correctly, it's a way to have yourself live on the slide as you present. A lot of video courses do this. Now it's an option built right into PowerPoint. As you might have noticed on my own videos that I've done for Excel, I don't do that personally. But you do you and now you can.

* * *

Okay. Now let's go in depth on the more common objects you might want to insert into a slide, starting with Tables.

Tables

To insert a table into a slide, the first option is to click on the icon for a table in an existing text frame. The icon currently looks like a three-by-three grid with a darker bar across the top. Or you can go to the Insert tab and click on Table from there. Here you can see both of the options:

If you click on the table icon in a text frame, you'll see the Insert Table dialogue box which lets you specify a number of columns and rows to start with.

If you click on the Table option in the Insert tab, the dropdown menu will appear and you'll see a grid under the heading Insert Table.

Hold your mouse over any box in that grid and you'll see a table appear in the current slide that has that number of rows and columns. Also, the text above the grid will change to tell you the dimensions of the grid you're about to insert.

Click on that box in the grid to actually insert your table.

Another option is to click on Insert Table under that grid to bring up the Insert Table dialogue box.

You also can choose to Draw Table or insert an Excel Spreadsheet from that dropdown menu, although I don't personally use either of those often.

Don't worry too much about the number of rows, because those are easy to add. But do try to get the number of columns correct up front, it just makes life easier.

Okay then. Here I have inserted a 4 x 4 table into my slide:

I also reopened the Insert Table dialogue box so you could see what that looks like.

From this point you just need to add your text and format the table. I usually add text first, but either way works.

Add Text

The easiest way to add text to a table is to click into one of the cells in the table and start typing.

To move to the next cell over, use the Tab key. If you need to go back one cell, use Shift + Tab.

If you use Tab at the end of a row, it will take you to the first cell of the next row. If you're in the last row of the table, it will add another row for you and take you to the first cell of that new row. If you didn't want that new row, the easiest fix is to use Ctrl + Z to undo.

Arrows do work in tables, but in different ways depending on where you are at the time you try to use them. Right and left arrows will move you to the next cell in that direction if you have no text in the current cell.

If you do have text in that cell then you need to be at the beginning of the text to move left one cell or at the end of the text to move right one cell. Otherwise the arrows will move you through the contents of the current cell one letter at a time.

Same with up and down arrows which will move you to the cell above or below if there's no text, but will move you up or down one row if there is.

(This is why I just tend to use the Tab keys or click into the cell I want.)

Usually in PowerPoint I enter my data directly into each cell. Somehow that's easiest for me.

But you can also paste in text from Word, Excel, another slide, etc. To do so, use Ctrl + C to copy your text from wherever it is, click into the cell where you want to place that text, and then either use Ctrl + V to paste or use one of the Paste Options available in the Clipboard section of the Home tab or by right-clicking on the cell in the table.

If the text you copy and paste is not already in a table format, then all of that text is going to paste directly into that one cell of your table.

If you select multiple cells before you paste, it will just paste that text multiple times, all of the text once per selected cell.

So if I have "test, test, test" on three separate lines in Word, and I paste those three lines of text into a table in PowerPoint, I will get a single cell in my table that has all three lines of text.

If you want what you paste into PowerPoint to paste into multiple cells instead, then you need to copy from a Word table or an Excel file that has the data separated already.

And you need to either click into the first cell where you want to paste your data or you need to select the correct number of cells in your PowerPoint table to correspond to the size of the source table.

If you select too many cells to paste into, PowerPoint will repeat your entries to fill the selected space.

If you don't select enough cells to paste into, PowerPoint will only paste in what fits into the cells you've selected.

The best way to see this is just try it. Write a few lines of text in Word and then try to paste them in, do the same with a few entries in different cells in Excel. And then try pasting them into a PowerPoint table with different numbers of cells selected each time.

Another thing to watch out for if you're pasting in values from elsewhere is that you may lose the text formatting in PowerPoint and have to fix that.

When dealing with numbers that have formatting, it can sometimes be much easier to do all of the calculations and formatting outside of PowerPoint and then just paste in the results. PowerPoint does have that Excel spreadsheet option, too, but for me when I just used it, the table it ended up inserting had zero formatting. I'd rather copy and paste from an Excel file and use the formatting that's already in a default table for a theme than try to use an Excel worksheet embedded in a presentation and have to do ALL the formatting to match the theme.

Which you prefer really comes down to where your strengths are. Excel is my #1 program so I'm far more comfortable there.

If you do want to use the insert Excel worksheet option in PowerPoint then let me give you a few tips.

First, when I click on that option it inserts a very small Excel window with only Cells A1 through B2 visible. To make that bigger and more workable, left-click and drag from a corner. Your cursor will be angled and have arrows at both ends when you're positioned to do that.

You can then enter data into those cells just like you would with a normal Excel spreadsheet. The menu tabs up top will show as Excel options while you have that open:

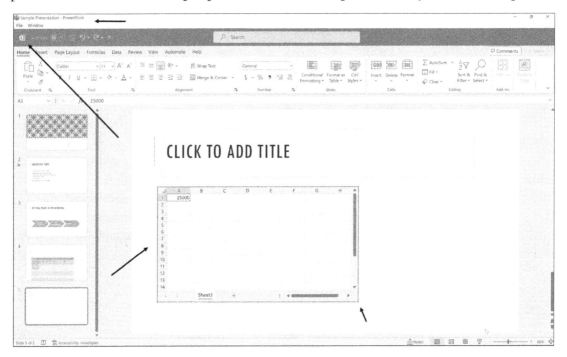

It's probably going to be a little hard to see in print, but at the top left corner right now I have the PowerPoint menu that still shows File and Window, but below that is all Excel. Those tabs for Home, Insert, Page Layout, etc. are the choices you see in Excel not PowerPoint.

So you can use any of those formatting or other options up there just like you would in Excel.

When you're done entering data, click away from that box and you'll have a table where the number of columns and rows matches however many rows and columns you made visible when you expanded your table:

See what I mean by lack of formatting? And PowerPoint treats this as a shape not a table so you need to go back into Excel to format the table.

To do so, double-click on that image to open it back up as an Excel worksheet. You can then use the Excel options to format the table. Any formatting you do when it's open as an Excel worksheet will remain when you click away again:

Here I added some shading in the first row, added borders around all cells and formatted the currency entry. But I also had to be careful to constrain my Excel view to just the cells I wanted to include on the slide.

It's…eh. It helps with number formatting or formulas, but it's a little fiddly to work with. So, enough of that. Let's pretend that you're just going to work with a basic table in PowerPoint instead.

When you insert a table and are clicked onto that table, there are going to be two new menu tabs available to you, Table Design and Layout:

Table Design lets you make your table pretty or fancy by choosing different colors, border styles, etc. Layout lets you control the more basic format of the table including number and size of rows and columns.

Let's start with the options available under Layout. I'll also mention as we go along other ways to make these changes.

Layout Options

It's very rare to have a table where all of the columns are the same width and all of the rows are the exact same height, so chances are you'll want to make some adjustments like that for any table you insert. Most of those options can be found on the Layout tab:

Let's walk through them now.

Column Width

To change the width of a column in a table, you have a few options.

The easiest, to me, is to hold the cursor over the edge of the column until the cursor looks like two parallel perpendicular lines with arrows pointing to each side. Left-click and drag the column border until the column is the width you want.

The total width of the table will not change, which means the neighboring column you drag towards or away from is going to also adjust in width to maintain the total width of the table.

Here you can see that I made Column 1 skinnier and this had the impact of making Column 2 wider. (I started with all columns the same width as Column 3):

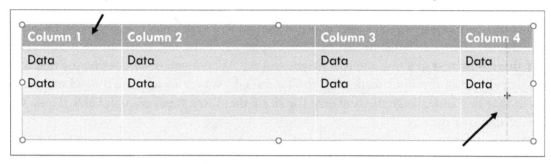

You can also see that I'm in the process of changing the width of Column 4—see the dotted line and the cursor that looks like those two parallel perpendicular lines with arrows pointing left and right.

With that Column 4, because it's the edge of the table, changing that column width from the edge will also change the overall width of the table.

(This example used those two parallel lines with arrows pointing to either side, but actually the easiest way to click and drag from the outer edges of a table to change a column width, is to go to the white circle along that edge and left-click and drag while the cursor looks like a white arrow pointing left and right.)

You can see the white circles along the edge of the table above. They're generally at the middle of each edge and the corners.

Another option for changing your Column Width is to click on a cell in the column you want to change, go to the Cell Size section of the Layout tab, and change the Width value there:

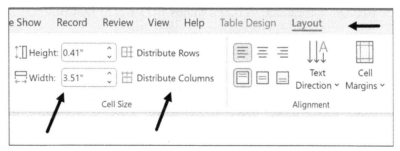

If you want all of your columns to have the same width, click into the table and then click on the Distribute Columns option in the Cell Size section of the Layout tab. The table width will not change, but all of your columns will adjust so that they are equal widths.

Row Height

Adjusting your row height works much the same way as adjusting your column width, with one small exception. Your row height is always going to automatically change to at a minimum fit the contents of your cells. You cannot have hidden text in a table in PowerPoint.

How this works is if you try to set your row height to a very small value, the row height will automatically change to a height that can still display all of the text from the cells in that row.

If there is no text in a row, the row height will stay tall enough to fit one row of text in the font size shown in the Font section of the Home tab. Which means you'd need to select all cells in that row and change the font size for all of them to a small enough value if you want to make that row shorter.

So.

Option one for changing the row height is to position the cursor over the top or bottom border for that row, and then left-click and drag to the size you want.

Option two is to go to the Cell Size section of the Layout tab and change the Height value for that row that you're clicked into.

And, technically, a third option for changing row height is to change the font size for all of the cells in that row when that row has no text in it.

To make all of your rows the same height, click into the table and use the Distribute Rows option from the Cell Size section of the Layout tab.

Changing the height of a single row does not impact the height of the row above or below it. But it will change the overall height of the table.

Keep in mind as you add text to a cell in your table, your row height will change to accommodate that text. This is why I usually save setting my column widths and row heights for the end after I have all of my text in. It lets me decide whether I'd rather make a column a little bit wider to get all of the text on one or two rows, or whether I'm fine with a row that is taller than the surrounding rows because the text in that cell wrapped around to a new line. I can also decide to change font size to make things fit better at that point.

Insert Columns

To insert an additional column into your table, click into a cell next to where you want to insert the column, and then go to the Rows & Columns section of the Layout tab and choose either Insert Left or Insert Right, as appropriate.

The overall width of your table will remain unchanged, so inserting a column will impact the width of all of the other columns in your table. This is why I try to get the number of columns right from the start. Less formatting hassle.

The width of the inserted column is generally going to be the same as the width of the column that you were clicked into when you chose to insert it, but both will have proportionately adjust to accommodate that new column.

So, for example, right now I inserted a column into a table while clicked into a column that was 2.33 inches wide. My new column is the same width as the old column, but they are both now 1.86 inches wide because every column in the table had to shrink some to fit that new column.

You can also click into a cell, right-click, and choose Insert Left or Insert Right from the mini formatting menu if those choices are available. That menu is dynamic, so they may not be.

Insert Rows

The easiest way to insert a new row at the bottom of your table is to just go to the end of the far right cell in the last row and use the Tab key.

You can also click into a cell in the table where you want the new row to be inserted, and then go to the Rows & Columns section of the Layout tab, and choose Insert Above or Insert Below. The row that is inserted will be the same height as the *default* height of the row you were clicked into.

Inserting a new row will change the overall height of the table. No other row heights will be affected but watch that the new row doesn't take your table off the page. (If it does, try making the table wider to fit more text on a line or change your font size to fit more text. You can't click and drag from the corner to adjust it.)

Delete Columns or Rows

To delete a column or row, you can select the entire row or column and then use the Backspace key. (Using the Delete key will remove any text but leave the actual column or row in place.)

Your other option is to click into a cell in that row or column, go to the Rows & Columns section of the Layout tab, and then click on the dropdown under Delete and choose to Delete Columns or Delete Rows from there.

Delete Table

To delete an entire table, you can use the Delete Table option in that Delete dropdown in the Rows & Columns section of the Layout tab which we just saw.

Or you can select the whole table when your cursor looks like four arrows pointing left and right and up and down, and then use either the Backspace or Delete key.

Select Table

I usually select a table by using the cursor when it's pointing in all four directions, but sometimes that's annoying to get working. It usually requires putting your cursor somewhere along the outer edge of the table.

Another option is to click anywhere on the table, go to the Layout tab, and then use the dropdown under Select in the Table section on the far left to Select Table.

With either of those options it won't look like anything happened, but if you use Backspace or Delete the table will be deleted.

Select Row or Column

I usually just left-click and drag to select all of the cells in a row or column.

But you can also click into a cell in the table that's in that row or column, and then go to the Table section of the Layout tab, and choose Select Column or Select Row from the Select dropdown menu.

Selected cells will be grayed out in comparison to other cells in the table.

Merge or Split Cells

It is possible to merge or split selected cells within a table. I always save this for as long as I can if I'm going to do it, because it makes the rest of your formatting more difficult to do.

Here is an example of a table that uses this sort of formatting:

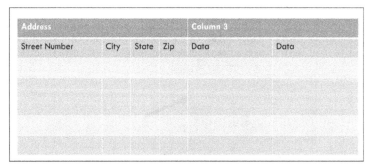

Note how the number of columns differs across rows? The first row only has two columns. The second row and all those after it have six columns.

A table like this can either be built from merging cells, so in this case I'd start with six columns and then merge the cells in that first row. Or it can be built my splitting cells, so in this case I'd start with two columns and then break those up into four columns and two columns, respectively, for the rest of the rows.

In a table like this, if you add a new row it will have the same number of columns as the row you were clicked into when you added the new row. So once this is set up I can go to the very bottom cell of that table, use Tab, and have another row with six columns in it.

To merge cells together, select the cells you want to merge, go to the Merge section of the Layout tab, and click on Merge Cells. The selected cells will all become one cell and any text in those cells will be brought into that one cell starting with the top left cell, going across that row, and then left to right for any additional rows of cells that were merged.

And, yes, you can merge across columns and down rows at once.

Another way to merge cells is to right-click after selecting your cells and choose Merge Cells from the dropdown menu.

Split Cells works in a similar way. Select the cells you want to split and then either right-click and choose Split Cells or choose Split Cells from the Merge section of the Layout tab.

Split Cells can be applied to a single cell, but usually I want it for a range of cells in one column.

Both split cell options will bring up the Split Cells dialogue box. It has fields for the number of columns and number of rows you want your selection split into.

Each selected cell will be split according to your choice. So don't enter the total number of columns and rows you want to end up with. That's not how it works. If you have four cells selected and you choose two columns in the Split Cells dialogue box, you will end up with eight columns. Four cells, each split in two.

Which means if you work with Split Cells sometimes it takes a little math or experimentation to get the appearance you want. And sometimes it's better to just select one column or one row and work from that or to merge everything and then split it if you don't have content in those cells yet.

One final note, when you split cells, the text stays in the top left-most cell of the group created out of that cell. So if I split a single cell into three rows and three columns, the text will be in the top left cell and the other eight cells I created will be empty. If I did that to two cells at once, each grouping of nine cells would have the text that was there before for that cell in the top leftmost cell of each cluster of nine.

It may sound confusing. It is a bit. If you need to do this, experiment and remember that Ctrl + Z, Undo, is your friend.

Text Alignment

As with most table designs, you may decide that you don't want your text in the default position, which is left-aligned and top aligned. Often, for example, for columns with numbers that are providing a count of entries, I will center the values. For currency values, I may prefer to right-align.

You have nine total alignment choices because there are three choices about how you align text left to right and three choices about how you align text top to bottom. (We'll cover text direction, which is another choice, next.)

Here is a table with nine cells in it that uses each combination:

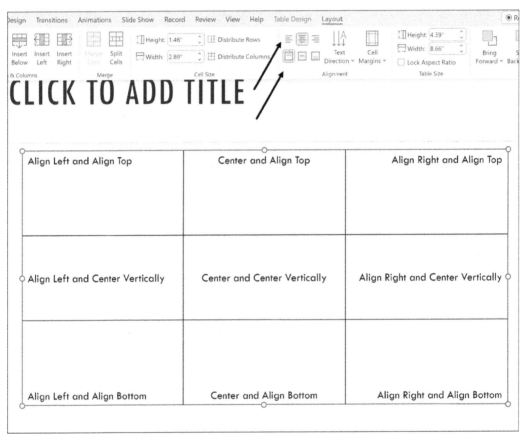

The alignment options that I used are available in the Alignment section of the Layout tab. The top row of choices gives you Align Left, Center, and Align Right. In the row below that you can choose from Align Top, Center Vertically, and Align Bottom. Each option shows text that is aligned in that manner.

The screenshot above has Center and Align Top selected. They have light gray boxes around them to show that they're the current selections.

Sometimes you won't see the difference between two choices, because the column is too narrow or the row height is too short to show the difference. That's why I always wait to make this choice until I've added all of my text and finalized my column widths and row heights.

The left, center, and right options should always be available in the mini formatting menu. Top, center, and bottom may or may not be available.

To apply alignment, just select your cells and then make your choice.

Text Direction

With all of those choices we just walked through, the text was still left-to-right. It was just a matter of changing where it fell within that cell.

But you can also change the direction of the text in a cell. Those options can be found under the Text Direction dropdown menu in the Alignment section of the Layout Tab. Here we go:

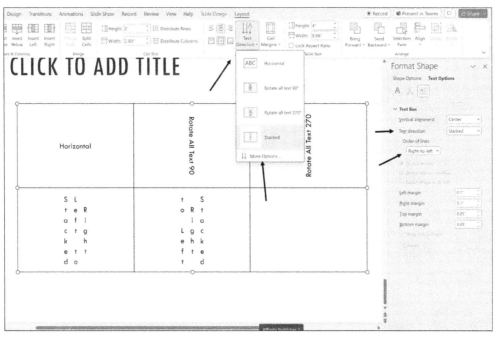

There is a More Options choice at the bottom of that text direction dropdown. Clicking on it will bring up the Format Shape task pane on the right-hand side of your workspace which you can see above. The Text Direction dropdown menu there has the same four choices.

Horizontal is the top left example in that table there. It's the default. The next cell in that table shows the rotate all text ninety degrees option. The next cell shows the rotate two hundred and seventy degree option.

Your final option is Stacked. You can see examples in the bottom row of the table above.

Stacked puts the letters one on top of each other from top to bottom until it reaches the bottom of the cell and then it starts a new column. Note that it will start a new column mid-word, so you need to pay attention when using it.

The default is stacked left-to-right but in the Format Shape pane you can choose right-to-left instead.

For me, personally, I use Horizontal primarily but will sometimes use Rotate All Text 270 if I have merged cells along the left-hand edge of a table.

Cell Margins

For the most part, you should be able to leave this setting alone. It can be found in the Alignment section of the Layout tab. The dropdown menu for Cell Margins will show four options or you can choose to customize your settings.

Use cell margins in situations where your text is going too close to the edge of the cell or not close enough.

Table Size

You can manually set the size of your table in the Table Size section of the Layout tab. By default, though, you will be constrained by the contents of the table, especially when setting your height value.

The way around this is to check the box for Lock Aspect Ratio first. If you do that, then you can change the height to a smaller value than the contents would normally allow, and PowerPoint will adjust the font size to make that work.

You can also click on a table and then click and drag from one of the white circles around the edges to change a table size, but the Layout menu option with Lock Aspect Ratio is probably the best way to do this.

The Format Shape task pane also has a setting for table size.

Table Design Options

Now let's turn our attention to the Table Design tab where you can make your table look pretty.

Table Styles

Table Styles are pre-formatted options for your table design. There are seven different color options:

Click on the downward-pointing arrow on the bottom right of that section (noted in the screenshot above) and you'll see that there are a lot of styles to choose from within each color group:

Across each row the design is the same, but down each column is a different color.

In this presentation theme, the left column is black/white/gray and but the other columns use blues or greens. The colors here will vary depending on presentation theme.

The options are split between Best Match for Document, Light, Medium, and Dark. Personally, I think that "Best Match for Document" category does not show a very good understanding of what I'm doing, but honestly, the category names really don't matter. Just find the one that looks the most like what you want.

You can hold your mouse over each of the options to see it applied to your table. Click if you want to keep it.

I do think it's best to add text to the table first before doing this. Of course, for me these styles are never quite what I'm looking for, but they can be a good place to start.

Table Style Options

Once you get close to what you want, you can then customize from there using the checkboxes in the Table Style Options section:

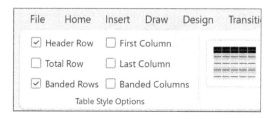

You can see that right now the Header Row and Banded Row options are checked for my table. And this is what that looks like:

Note two things. The first row of this table is a different color. That's what happens when the Header Row box is checked.

Second, the remaining rows in the table alternate between two colors, one darker and one lighter. That's Banded Rows.

If I want to turn both of those off and not have them in my table, I can just uncheck those boxes. And here we go:

Pretty ugly, huh?

What about the other choices there? Total Row will make the last row of the table a different color. First Column will make the first column of the table a different color. Last Column, you guessed it, makes the last column a different color. Here are all three applied at once:

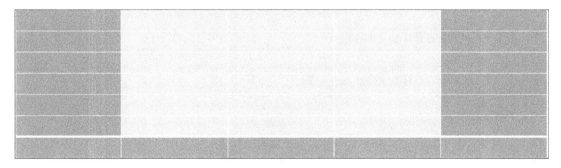

Doesn't really work, does it?

Note, too, that for the Total Row the border directly above that row is slightly thicker. The same thing happens for the Header Row where the border below is slightly thicker.

Finally, there is an option for Banded Columns that does for columns what Banded Rows does for rows. It makes every other main body column a different color.

I would recommend not having banded rows and columns together, because that creates a checkerboard appearance in every other column which looks weird.

The point of banded rows and columns is to let you scan over or down more easily. So if your user is going to primarily be reading across the table, use banded rows. If they're going to be primarily reading down a column in the table, use banded columns. For smaller tables you may not need either one.

And again, I'd recommend having your text in your table first before you make these choices.

Shading

You can also manually apply your own color to cells in the table using the Shading option. To do so select the cells you want to change, and then go to the Shading dropdown menu in the Table Styles section of the Table Design tab:

Click on the color you want to apply. You can hold your mouse over each color to see what it will look like before you make your choice.

To stay compatible with your template, it's best to keep within those first seventy color options which will be customized to the template.

But you can also choose one of the Standard Colors, or click on More Fill Colors to bring up the Colors dialogue box which lets you specify a custom color or choose from pretty much any color that exists.

There are some other options in that dropdown like Picture, Gradient, and Texture that we're not going to cover here in detail. They do exist if you really want to go there, I'd just remind you that your presentation exists to support what you're saying not to steal the show from you.

That dropdown is also where you can choose No Fill to remove a color from your selected cells.

And there's an Eyedropper option there that will let you choose a color from another element in your presentation.

Borders

By default, your theme will probably already use some sort of border. In this example that I've been working with, the borders are white and go around every cell by default. But you can change that.

Select the cells where you want to apply your borders and then use the dropdown for Borders in the Table Styles section of the Table Design tab to select the type of border you want:

Now, there's a 50/50 chance that you didn't like something about the border you just applied. Chances are it's because of the color of the line or the width of the line.

To fix that, you need to Undo and then go to the Draw Borders section of the Table Design tab. In that section you can change the type of line, the width (point size) of the line, or the color (pen color) of the line:

Nothing will change after you make your choices until you then go back and apply the border to those cells again. You can click on each line you want to change while your cursor looks like a little pen or you can use Esc to turn that off and then select your range of cells to format and use the Borders dropdown menu once more.

Here I changed my line color and width and then used the All Borders option on every cell in my table:

I think I'd need to see data in there to see if it works, but you get the idea. I'd probably ultimately keep that thicker blue border around the perimeter and the top and bottom rows but go with something more subtle for the data rows in the interior.

Sometimes when working with borders it takes a few different tries or multiple applications of borders to get the look you want. I often like to have a thicker outer border around a table and then a thinner border around the cells in the table itself, for example, which requires application of two different sets of borders to the same cells.

Effects

No.

You can see below the Borders dropdown in the Table Styles section of the Table Design tab that there is an option for Effects. This lets you apply bevels, shadows, and reflections to cells in your table or your entire table. Maybe don't?

I mean, I'm sure there's a reason this menu exists. I think it's more useful when working with WordArt or Shapes, though. So I'm just going to tell you not to do it. But if you want to do it, select your cells, go to the option you want, hold your mouse over each one to see what it will look like, and then click to apply.

WordArt Quick Styles

Same with WordArt. You could apply it to the text in your table. I'm sure there have been times when someone did and it worked. But for your standard business presentation? Eh. I'd say leave it alone. Better used on the first page of a presentation or in the title field. Or for when you're creating something like a book cover in PowerPoint. (Although there are better programs for that and some are even free. Email me if you need recommendations.)

Again, though, if you want it, select the text in your table you want to apply it to, hold your mouse over the options under the Quick Styles dropdown to see what your text will look like, and then click to apply. To customize your appearance, use the Text Fill, Text Outline, and Text Effects dropdowns next to that.

Font Color

There is one useful option in that WordArt Styles section of the Table Design tab, and that's the top dropdown there for Text Fill. Choosing a color from that dropdown should change the font color of your selected text.

Personally, I use the Font Color option in the Font section of the Home tab instead, because I am a creature of habit. The mini formatting menu will also work. As will right-clicking, choosing Font from the dropdown menu, and changing the Font Color in the Font dialogue box.

Draw Table

The Draw Table option in the Draw Borders section of the Table Design tab is another way to split columns or rows. It was a little temperamental for me, but I was able to get it to work.

Make sure your line type, width, and color are what you want before you start, and then click on Draw Table. Your cursor should look like a pen.

Left-click somewhere within the cell where you want to draw a new border, but not on the edges of the cell. Hold that left-click and drag to draw a line. That should split that cell into either two columns or two rows depending on the line you drew.

You can only split a row if it's tall enough to accommodate two lines of text already.

Be careful, because if you click and drag from the edge of a cell instead, it will draw a new table on top of your existing table that's one cell wide by one cell tall.

As long as your cursor looks like a pen, you can keep drawing lines. Click on Draw Table again if it turns itself off.

When you're done, use Esc to turn the tool off.

Eraser

The Eraser tool, which is also in the Draw Borders section of the Table Design tab, lets you remove lines from a table. Click on it and then click directly on the line you want to take away.

You may be left with a black line around the perimeter if you erase a perimeter line, but that's just there to indicate the boundaries of your table. If you bring up the presentation slide you'll see that there's actually no line in that spot on the presentation.

Be careful with this one, because I was able to create a scenario where it removed the line between two cells so they appeared as if they were one column, but they remained two separate cells. But in other examples I was able to erase the line and have it act like I'd merged those cells. So test your result.

Use Esc to turn it off when you're done.

Move Table

You will probably find that sometimes you accidentally move the table around when what you really wanted was to change a column width or row height. Ctrl + Z to Undo is probably the best choice in those instances. But, if you want to manually change the location of a table, either Select the table or click onto the table when the cursor is a four-sided black arrow, and then left-click and drag the table to where you need it.

To center your table on the slide, you can click on the table and then use the Align dropdown menu in the Arrange section of the Layout tab. Choose Align Center to align it left-to-right or Align Middle to align it top-to-bottom.

Keep in mind with Align Middle that you may have a title section on your slide and PowerPoint will not take that into account. By default it is going to align to the overall slide. So manually positioning the table may work better in that scenario.

Pictures

Next up is inserting pictures. In a text box you will usually have an icon for Stock Images and one for Pictures. Pictures is for when you're using an image from your own collection.

The Images section of the Insert tab also has a Pictures option where you can choose between This Device, Stock Images, and Online Pictures.

This chapter is for Pictures from This Device. I already mentioned Stock Images and the risks around using those. Copyright applies to all images you didn't take yourself, so be aware of those restrictions. I have a lot of photos I have paid to use over time, but even though they are on my device I still need to know which ones I'm allowed to use when. There are often limits on how long you can wait before you use an image and/or on how many copies of a product can be sold before that license becomes invalid.

Insert

Okay, lecture over. Click on This Device or the Picture icon in your text box. Either one will open the Insert Picture dialogue box.

Navigate to the image you want to use, click on it, and then click on Insert.

That Insert option has a dropdown that will let you choose to Link to File or Insert and Link instead. This can be useful if you have images that might get updated later and you want the presentation to automatically update.

But there are risks there, too. If you choose Link to File and you move that file or try to open the presentation on another computer that can't link to that file, you won't have that image in your presentation. It will be a blank box with an error message in it.

When I inserted my image into my presentation slide, PowerPoint brought up the Designer task pane on the right-hand side with all sorts of formatting suggestions for the slide:

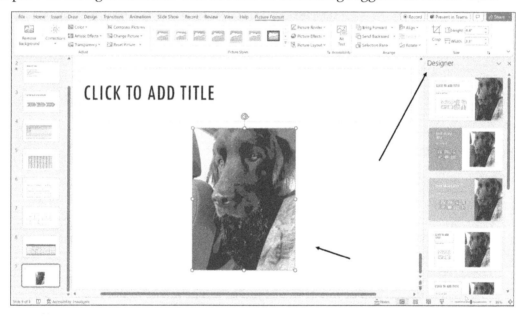

You can see the slide as it is now in the center. It just has my image (of my dog who I loved very much) with a title field above. Pretty boring and basic.

On that right-hand side the Designer is showing layouts that use that image and have a title section but also have another text box where I could put more content.

If you like one of those layouts, click on it to use it.

Another thing to note here, my photo adjusted to fit that text box. It's at 47% of its actual size right now.

Also, the text box changed size to match my photo's dimensions. By default, any photo you bring into a text box will either be fit to the height or width of the box, in this case the height, and then the other dimension will adjust so that the box is exactly the size of the picture.

When you're clicked onto an image inserted into your presentation, you will see a Picture Format tab with a number of adjustment options. Here you can see the left-hand set of choices:

Here are the right-hand set of options:

Let's now walk through what you can do with these.

Resize

The easiest way to change the size of a picture is to left-click and drag from the corner of the image. By default the image will scale up or scale down as you drag, keeping the height and width proportionate. So if you just want to eyeball your measurements, that's the way to go.

But sometimes you want all of your images to be an exact height or an exact width. When that's the case, click on the image and then go to the Size section of the Picture Format tab and change the Height or Width value there by clicking into one of those two boxes and typing the value you want.

By default that will also scale proportionately. (Which is generally what you want, because if you don't scale proportionately your image distorts and doesn't look like it should.)

You can use the expansion arrow in that Size section to open the Format Picture task pane and then uncheck Lock Aspect Ratio if you don't want that.

The Format Picture task pane also has a Reset option that will change the image back to its original size. Not the size it originally came into PowerPoint, but its original size before you imported it. For me with this image, that would be 9.26 inches by 6.94 inches which is too big for the slide.

Best Scale for Slide Show, which is another option, was also a bad idea in my case.

Move

Sometimes when you rescale an image, it moves around a bit. When that happens you will want to move the image back into place. The easiest way to do this is to left-click on the image when your cursor looks like a four-sided black arrow and then drag the image back into place.

As you left-click and drag the image around, look for very faint dotted lines that will appear as you align with different elements on the slide. For example, with a slide that has a title text frame it shows me when the image is aligned to the left edge, the center, and the right edge of that text frame as well as the top edge, middle, and bottom edge.

If you still have your Format Picture task frame open, you can also expand the Position section under Size & Properties and specify an exact position relative to the top left corner or the center of the slide. (This can be useful if you have images in the same exact position on consecutive slides and you want them to be in exactly the same spot on each slide.)

Another option is the Align dropdown menu in the Arrange section of the Picture Format tab. Choose the alignment you want from there.

Alt Text

For a presentation that you are giving to an audience, you probably won't need alt text. But if you're doing a PowerPoint presentation that is going to be circulated to others and watched online, then it may be useful to use.

PowerPoint makes an attempt to add alt text when an image is imported. If you ever need to see and/or edit that text, right-click on the image and choose View Alt Text from the dropdown menu.

This opens a task pane for Alt Text on the right-hand side of your workspace:

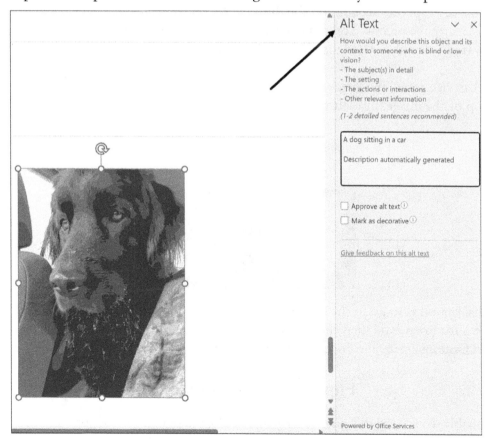

You can see here that it described my image as "A dog sitting in a car" which is accurate. Now, if I'd been using this image to demonstrate how to posterize an image, I might want to change that to something like "Posterized image of dog sitting in car". Or if I'd been demonstrating something about black dogs, I might need to add that it's a black dog. Or a Newfoundland. What Alt Text you put depends on the reason for using the image.

You can see here that it also included a note that this was an automatically generated description which tells a user it may not be a good description for purposes of this presentation. You can approve that alt text by checking the approval box below the description. Or you can edit the text by clicking into the text box and making changes. If the image you imported is just there for decoration and doesn't need to be described, click the Mark As Decorative box.

Rotate

Sometimes a picture comes in sideways or maybe you want to rotate it for other reasons.

One way to do this is to go to the Format Picture task pane and enter a value for Rotation in the Size & Properties section. It's the third choice under Size.

That lets you be precise. You can enter 90 or 270 to rotate the image right or left by ninety degrees. If you already rotated the image and want it back to where it started, change the value to zero.

You can also rotate the image directly on your slide. There is a little looping arrow usually at the top of the image. Just left-click on that and drag:

Your final option is to go to the Arrange section of the Picture Format tab and click on the dropdown for Rotate and then choose to Rotate Right 90 or Rotate Left 90. Clicking on More Rotation Options opens the Format Picture task pane.

Flip Vertical or Horizontal

You probably won't need this one, but if you ever do, under that Rotate option in the Arrange section of the Picture Format tab there are two other choices, Flip Vertical and Flip Horizontal:

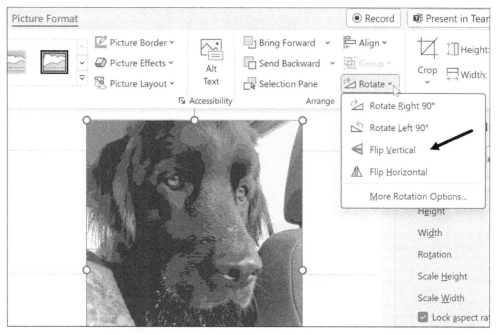

Here, I have flipped the image horizontally. Notice how the dog now faces to the right instead of the left. If I were to flip vertically the dog's head would be at the bottom of the image.

Be careful if you flip an image that there isn't text in the image because the text will be backwards or upside down.

Crop

Sometimes you bring in a picture and don't want all of the image. To fix that you can crop your image. The option is available in the Size section of the Picture Format tab. Click on Crop or in the dropdown menu there choose Crop.

That will place black markers at the corners and around the edge of your image. Left-click and drag on any of those black lines to crop from that spot inward.

Here you can see the grayed out area that will disappear if I accept the cropping I've done so far:

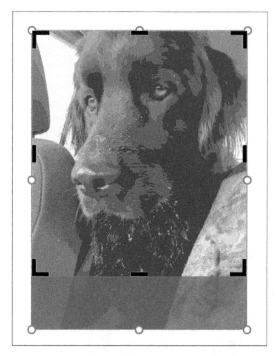

You won't see the black bars as you're dragging, they only reappear when you're done moving that black line.

You can crop more than one side at a time. Do the first one, let up on your left-click and then left-click and drag on the next bar.

When you're done, use Enter or Esc or click away to lock in your cropped image:

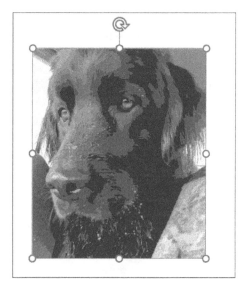

For any image that isn't fully visible on your slide, you can click on it, choose the Crop option, and then left-click and drag the image around to change what part of the image will be visible. You'll see the visible part in color and the parts that won't be visible grayed out.

Once you have the image positioned the way you want, click away, Esc, or Enter.

Note that there were other crop options in that dropdown like crop to shape that we're not going to cover here but that you can use to have your image appear in a star or circle or some other shape.

Another way to bring up the Crop option is to right-click and choose Crop from the mini formatting menu at the bottom of the dropdown menu.

Align

As we discussed with tables, there are also alignment options for pictures. You can align a picture to the left, center, right, top, middle, or bottom of the slide using the Align dropdown menu in the Arrange section of the Picture Format tab.

You can also align objects to one another.

I will sometimes if I have three or more pictures in a slide, select all of them and then use the Distribute Horizontally or Distribute Vertically options. This makes the space between the images equal and is easier than trying to do it manually.

It's also possible with multiple images to align them left, center, right, etc. to one another instead of to the slide. You just need to select them and, if it doesn't happen automatically, change the Align to Slide option at the bottom of the dropdown over to Align Selected Objects. After that you can choose the type of alignment you want. When you do this, the objects will align within the space created by their outermost edges. That means that sometimes to get the look I want I have to move the outermost object outward or inward to create the correct perimeter for PowerPoint to align within.

Bring Forward/Send Backward

You probably will not need this for most presentations. But if you ever have images or elements on the page that overlap one another, you can bring an element forward so that it's on top or send one backward so that it's underneath any other element.

To do so, click on that element and then go to the Arrange section of the Picture Format tab and choose Bring Forward or Send Backward. Those choices work to bring the element one layer forward or send it one layer backward.

In the dropdown choices for each, you also have the option to Bring to Front or Send to Back. That will place the element either all the way at the front or all the way at the back.

This really only comes into play when you have multiple overlapping elements, though. If everything is in its own space, no need to worry about this.

Picture Adjustments

PowerPoint has a number of options for image adjustments. For a standard presentation I don't expect you to need these so I'm going to run through them fast.

On the far left there is an option for Remove Background. If you click on that, it gives you a pen that you can use to select the parts of the image that you want to keep or another one for selecting areas to get rid of. I've had to use tools like this with book cover design projects and I have to say it's pretty decent. In about thirty seconds I was able to do this:

See how all the blanket and seat sections of the image are now gone but you can still see the individual hairs on her ears? Not bad.

So if there's something in your image that you don't want there, this may be the way to fix it.

Next to that is the Corrections dropdown menu:

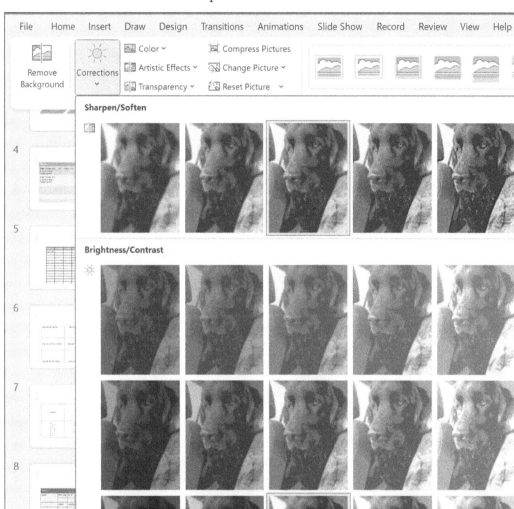

This lets you sharpen or soften an image or change the brightness and/or contrast. You can see what each one will look like in that dropdown. Just click on the one you want.

If you need more control, click on Picture Corrections Options at the very bottom and that will open the Format Picture task pane to the Picture Corrections options, which includes sliders for Sharpness, Brightness, and Contrast.

Next you have dropdowns for Color, Artistic Effects, and Transparency. Each dropdown has thumbnails of the image and what it will look like under each setting. Click on the one you want.

In the bottom of the next column of choices is an option to Reset Picture which lets you either reset the picture adjustments or, if you use the dropdown, reset the picture and its size. Just keep in mind that if you reset size you take the image back to its original size, which for me in this presentation was too large an image.

The Change Picture option there lets you choose a new picture to replace the current one. If you do so you will lose any adjustments you had made to the original picture.

Picture Styles

After the Adjust section in the Picture Format tab is the Picture Styles section. I generally don't use this much for business presentations, but I could see someone using it. There is a dropdown menu there with pre-formatted choices that let you apply frames or effects around your picture:

Off to the right side of those choices there are dropdowns for choosing a picture border or picture effects. You can refine a pre-formatted style using those options or create something from scratch.

Here I used the double frame option in the pre-formatted styles section but then I changed the border color over to match the slide:

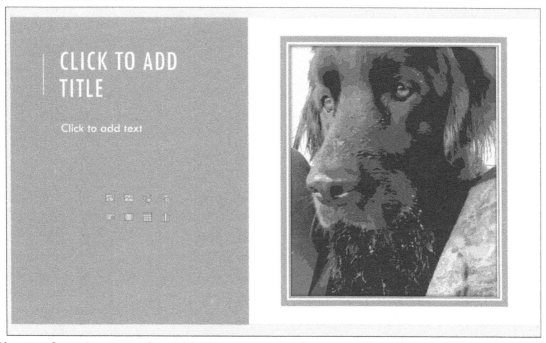

Plenty of options to play with. Just, once again, remember that the purpose of the presentation slides is to help you convey your message so don't let all the bells and whistles take over from what you're trying to do.

Picture Layout

There is a dropdown for Picture Layout in the Picture Styles section of the Picture Format tab. Ignore this one. It's for SmartArt which we'll cover shortly.

Videos

Now let's talk videos. I have seen many a presentation that had a video embedded. To do so, you can either click on the Insert Video option in a text box, which currently looks like a snippet of film, or you can go to the Insert tab and choose Video from the Media section at the far right of the Insert tab.

The dropdown options in the Insert tab are This Device, Stock Videos, and Online Videos.

For Online Videos, PowerPoint currently supports YouTube, SlideShare, Vimeo, Stream, and Flip. If you use online videos you are subject to each provider's terms of use and privacy policy, so be sure you know what you're doing. But you just give the address of the video and go from there.

If you use the Insert Video option from the text box on a slide the default is to find a video on your device.

I think most people who use videos will be pulling videos from somewhere like YouTube, so let's do that. First, go find the video you want to use. I have some Excel videos up on YouTube so I'm going to use one of those.

Once you find the video, copy the website address.

Next, go to the Insert tab and choose the Online Videos option from the dropdown menu for Video in the Media section. Paste in your address. It will show you a preview of the video:

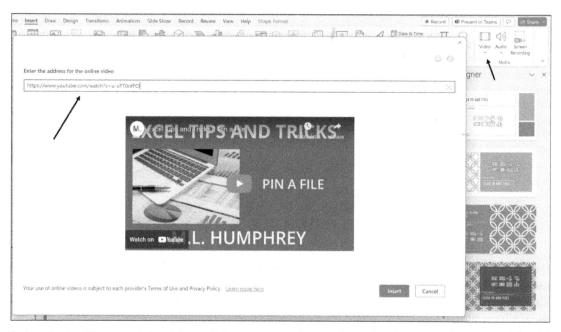

If that looks like the right video, click on Insert. The video will show on the slide with a big play button on it:

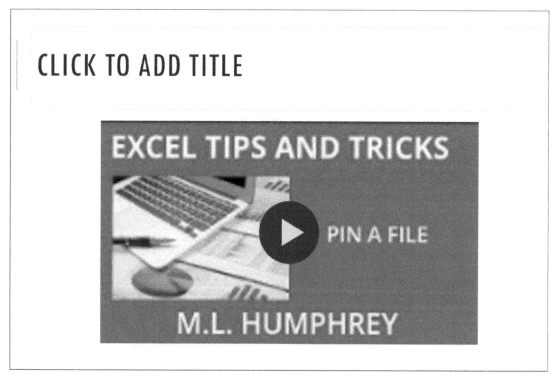

For me that inserted image looks pretty blurry, but when the video plays on the slide it looks okay.

If you instead insert a video from your own device, it will come up with the play bar below the image, like so:

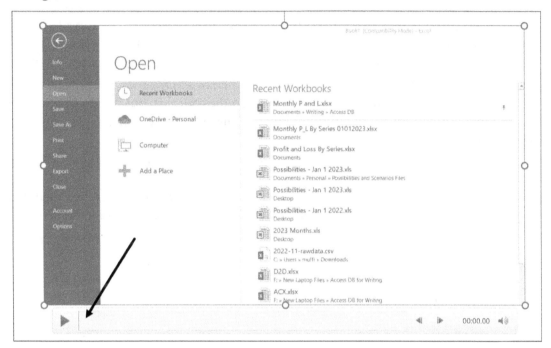

That's not the best thumbnail image it's showing, but it is the image that starts that video because this was the original video without any bells and whistles like a title image added. So keep that in mind if you use one of your own videos. Make sure the video has a good starting image.

Anyway. For either one, you just click the black triangle, wherever it is on the page, to play your video. During a live presentation you may need to hold your mouse over the video image to see it.

There are a number of options for formatting or editing a video after you insert it. Those options are available under the Video Format and Playback tabs that appear when the video is selected.

Video Format has Adjust and Video Styles sections that let you change the brightness or color of the video as well as apply poster frames or a shape to the video. There are also Accessibility (Alt Text), Arrange, and Size options that are similar to what we saw with Pictures.

The Playback tab really only works for your own videos. It has options that let you bookmark a section of the video, add a fade in or out, trim the video, or choose how the video is played or displayed. These options are largely grayed out if you insert a YouTube video, though, and I expect it's the same for other outside videos.

I'm not going to do a deep dive on videos, but a few points.

If you add a bookmark, that just lets you click to that point, it doesn't start the video at that point. For that you should probably trim the video.

You can set a video to play fullscreen.

You can also set a video to loop until stopped. This is a good way, for example, to have images that display on the screen while you're waiting to start your presentation. Make a simple little video with images of your company or your topic and set it to play until stopped.

If you want captions on your video, the format they need to be in is WebVTT. You'll have to upload that file separately. (You could also just generate a version of your video that has your captions embedded so that you don't have to go through this, but the drawback to that is they may overlap content in the video and can't be turned off. Most online platforms don't allow that type of video.)

You can choose when the video should start playing. Choices are automatically, when clicked on, or in click sequence.

And that's pretty much it. The big work on videos happens before you embed them most times. Once they're properly created, it really is usually just a matter of find it, embed it, and click to play.

SmartArt

Okay. Time to talk about one of my least favorite topics in PowerPoint but one that is used very often, especially in consulting contexts: SmartArt.

Theoretically, SmartArt is great. It lets you create these complex flow charts or diagrams that really illustrate what you're trying to say.

The reason I don't like SmartArt is because of how much I've seen it misused or abused. So, please, for the love of all that's holy, think when you use SmartArt.

Do these items belong together? Is this the right image to portray this relationship? What information do you need to include to show the relationship and what can be removed?

Really make sure that what you're doing makes sense. Because if it doesn't, you lose your audience. There is someone like me sitting there no longer listening to you because I don't understand why that pyramid has three completely unrelated items in it.

Rant over. Now let's walk through how to use this.

Insert

To insert SmartArt into your slide, either click on the Insert a SmartArt Graphic option from a text box, or click where you want to place it and then go to the Illustrations section of the Insert tab and click on SmartArt from there.

Both options will bring up the Choose a SmartArt Graphic dialogue box:

In the image above it is showing the Basic Block List. Note how there is a description on the right-hand side related to how to use this image. It says this image is for non-sequential or grouped blocks of information. So you wouldn't use this one for a process flow.

On the left-hand side of the dialogue box are categories of types of image. So if I have a product life cycle I want to illustrate, I could click on Cycle and see my choices:

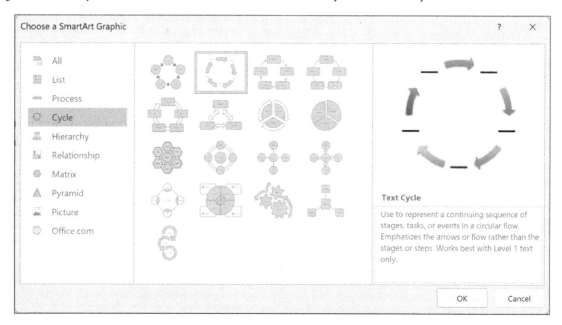

Here I've clicked on Text Cycle which it says should be used to represent a continuing sequence. It also says it works best with Level 1 text only, which means that you could have a label for each arrow, but wouldn't include subpoints or further details.

So the first step is to find the SmartArt that works for the information you want to present. Once you've done that and clicked on that option, click on OK to insert it into your slide. I'm going to go ahead and choose Basic Chevron Process. Here is what I get:

You can't see this in print, but the colors used for the graphic match my presentation theme.

Now we do all the work of adding and formatting this so it works for our purposes.

Add Text

The next step is to add text to the graphic.

When I inserted the graphic, PowerPoint automatically opened the SmartArt Design tab for me. In the top left corner of that tab there is an option for Text Pane. When I click on that, I get this Type Your Text Here dialogue box:

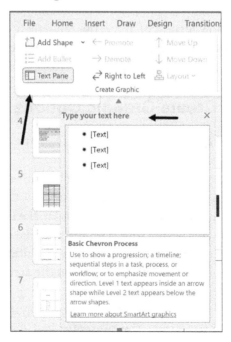

I can click into that dialogue box and replace those [Text] entries for each bullet point with my own text. Each bullet represents an element in the SmartArt, in this case a chevron.

If I need more elements than the three it started me with, I just use the enter key to add another bullet point.

As I add additional bullet points in the Text Pane, PowerPoint adds an element to the graphic and resizes all of the elements so they still fit on the slide. It also adjusts the font size so that the text fits on each element. Like so:

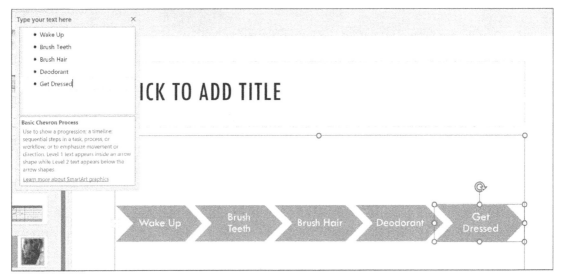

See how I have five chevrons now instead of three, but they still fit in the same space left-to-right.

You can also click directly onto an element and edit the text that way. That's often the easier choice if you just need to fix a typo or add/delete text from one element.

Create Graphic Options

In that same Create Graphic section of the SmartArt Design tab are some other options for customizing your SmartArt.

Add Shape will add another of that shape into the illustration.

Add Bullet will, in this case at least, add a bullet point *below* the selected design element.

Demote will remove an element from the graphic and make it into a bullet point below the graphic. Promote will take a bullet point from the slide and make it an element in the graphic.

Right to Left will change the direction the arrows are pointing in your graphic. The name of this one doesn't change depending on which direction the arrows are pointing, so just think of it as "change direction".

(By the way, this last week I saw a presentation that used a circular flow and did it counter-clockwise and my first thought was that the presenter had chosen chaos. This is probably cultural, but the default directions for information flow in the U.S. are going to be clockwise, left-to-right, and top-to-bottom.)

Move Up and Move Down move the selected element one spot up/left or one spot right/down in the SmartArt graphic.

Layouts

Next to the Create Graphic section in the SmartArt Design tab is the Layouts section. This section has a number of choices for that type of SmartArt. So here, for example, are various process layouts:

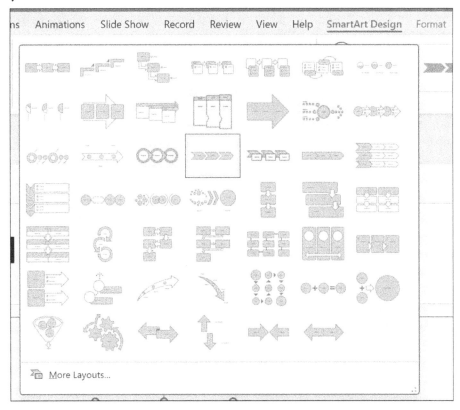

(By default you'll only see that top row of choices. Click on the downward-pointing arrow with a line in the bottom right corner to expand to see all choices like I did above.)

Here I changed the image over to another of the layout choices, but it still works because they're both process illustrations:

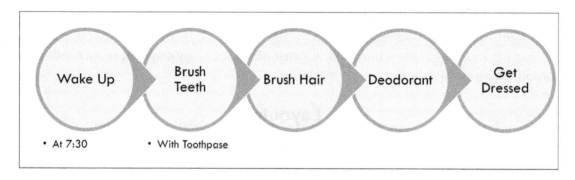

Change Colors

The next option in the SmartArt Design tab is the Change Colors dropdown menu in the SmartArt Styles section. If you don't like the color that PowerPoint chose for your SmartArt, you can change it here. Hold your mouse over each option to see it temporarily applied to your SmartArt and then click on the one you want.

Each Accent category is one color. Across the row for that accent category are the various format choices:

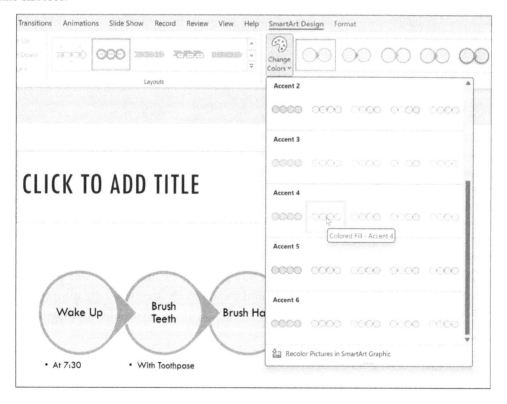

SmartArt Styles

The Change Colors option lets you change colors and style at the same time, but if those style options aren't quite what you want, there may be other choices available that work better in the SmartArt Styles section set of choices:

Once more you can click on the downward-pointing arrow with a line in the bottom right corner to see more choices. Or you can just arrow down to see one row of choices at a time.

For this specific layout the choices are pretty limited, honestly, but you can try them. Hold your mouse over each one to see what it will look like, click if you find one you want to use.

Reset Graphic

The Reset Graphic option in the Reset section of the SmartArt Design tab lets you take the SmartArt back to what it looked like before you did any special change of colors or SmartArt Styles. It retains the number of elements and text that you added, though.

Convert

The Convert option in the Reset section of the SmartArt Design tab lets you convert your SmartArt graphic to text or shapes.

For shapes it looks the same at first glance, but it's no longer SmartArt. Now it's just a series of shapes that you can still edit, but maybe not as easily. You can tell this by looking at the tab options up top which will have a Shape Format tab when you click on the image but no SmartArt Design and Layout tabs anymore.

For text it turns it into a bulleted list and removes all the images.

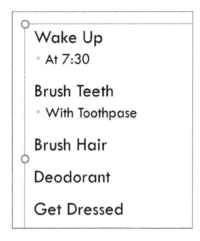

It is possible to take a bulleted list like this one above and convert it to SmartArt. Just select the text (Ctrl + A), right-click, choose Convert to SmartArt from the dropdown menu, and then choose the graphic you want to use:

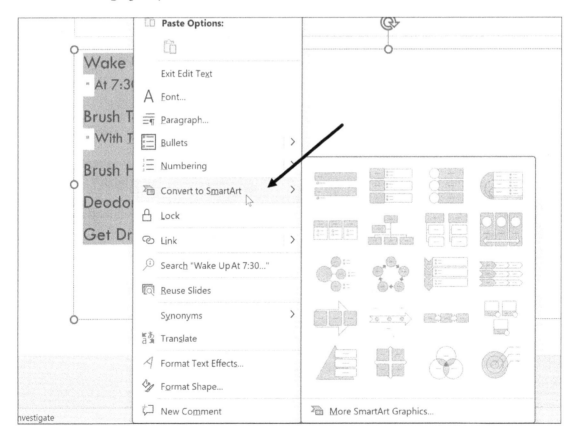

Format Elements and Text

The Format tab that appears for SmartArt is for changing the color, shapes, and effects for the elements in your SmartArt. It should look familiar by now because it's basically the same as for other items you can insert into a presentation slide.

To format your SmartArt, click on an element(s) and then you can apply whatever formatting you want to that element. (Use Ctrl + A to select all of the elements at once or use Shift or Ctrl as you click on each element you want to include.)

The default colors you see under the various options should be colors that are compatible with your presentation theme. So if you stick to those top 70 color swatches, especially if you stay within one row or one column, the elements in your SmartArt should work well visually with the rest of the elements in your presentation.

Depending on the element you have in your SmartArt, the Shape Fill and Shape Outline options may not do exactly what you want them to do. Same with the Change Shape option.

So if you want to make those sorts of changes, you may be better off working from the SmartArt Design tab and choosing a different layout instead. But you can experiment and see what's possible. Just remember that if something doesn't work Ctrl + Z, Undo, is your best friend because it's often easier to back away from a bad choice than try to move forward and fix it.

Okay. On to Shapes.

Shapes

You can add pretty much any shape you want to a PowerPoint slide. The other day I had to draw money flows for someone who had five bank accounts and ten places that money came from and another ten places the money went. None of the SmartArt was going to do that well. So I just created it from scratch using shapes.

I don't want to bog down in this too much, but I do want to at least cover the basics for you.

For me, working with shapes, I want a completely blank slide to work with. So if I have a template that has a title field and text field for the default slide, I add a new slide and then delete both.

To delete any element on a slide, click on it until you see the white circles around the perimeter, make sure you're not clicked into the box where you can add text, and then use Delete or Backspace.

Insert Shape

To insert a shape, go to the Insert tab and click on the dropdown under Shapes in the Illustrations section:

Click on the shape you want.

(There are even more choices that you can't see here, this is just the top of the dropdown menu. But it gives you a good feel for what you can add to your presentation slide.)

A few key shapes to discuss.

Text Box

That first option you can see there under Recently Used Shapes that has an A in a box and that's also visible in the Basic Shapes section, is the text box option.

If you want to add text, you need to use a text box.

Click on that option and then left-click and drag on your presentation slide to create your text box. There will be a cursor in the box, start typing to add your text.

By default, the height of the text box will match the text you enter into it. So it really doesn't matter how tall you make it to start, it's going to shrink down to your text. You can fix this after you add the text box by changing the height value in the Size section of the Shape Format tab.

Arrowed Lines

In the Lines section you can see a variety of line types. If you want to point from one spot to another, be sure to choose a line that has an arrow at one end (or both if that's what you need).

If you need a line that has a bend in it, choose the ones that show that in their thumbnail because a straight line can't be bent later

It works the same as a text box, click on your choice, and then left-click and drag on your slide to place the arrow where you need it.

For curved or bent lines, you can adjust the bend later by clicking on the line and then left-clicking and dragging the circles on the lines to change the shape. That's also how you can change the length or position of the endpoints for a straight line.

To move a line, left-click and drag the line while your cursor looks like arrows pointing in all four directions.

Other Shapes

There are obviously a lot of other shapes you can choose from in that dropdown menu. For each one, click on your choice in the Insert Shapes dropdown menu. For most you then left-click and drag to create the shape on the slide. For the scribble option, you left-click and drag to draw.

Once a shape is inserted into your slide its shape and dimensions can be changed by left-clicking on the image and then left-clicking and dragging the circles that appear along the lines that form the image. The only exception, I believe, is the scribble option which is set in the form you created, but can be resized like a photo by clicking and dragging from the edges.

Shape Styles

For every shape you add, there will be a Shape Format tab available when you are clicked onto that shape.

That tab has sections for Shape Styles and WordArt Styles. For the most part, you should already know how those work. For lines use the Shape Outline dropdown or Shape Styles options. For two-dimensional shapes use Shape Fill, Shape Outline, and the Shape Styles options.

Arrange Shapes

When adding a bunch of shapes to a slide you may find that some are on top of others and that you don't like one blocking out the other but you want both in that position. Or maybe you have three shapes on the slide and they don't quite line up visually even though you want them to.

The Arrange section of the Shape Format tab is where you need to go to fix those sorts of issues.

We already discussed a bit the Bring Forward/Send Backward options. Those are how you put one element in the foreground or move it to the background so that any element it overlaps is hidden behind it or shows on top of it.

Selection Pane will open the Selection task pane to let you see all of the elements on that slide. You can then lock an element so it can't be changed by clicking on the padlock shape or you can hide an element by clicking on the circle with a line arcing over the top:

Here for Connector: Curved 21 I've locked that shape and for Rectangle 24 I've hidden it. The other elements on the page are still capable of being seen and moved around.

In this case, it was easier to lock that one element and then go back to the slide and use Ctrl + A to select all of the other elements and align them to one another than it would have been to try to individually select each one.

With respect to aligning elements on the slide, if you select one element the default is to Align to Slide. If you select more than one element the default is to Align Selected Objects.

When you Align Selected Objects they align within the space covered by those elements. So imagine drawing a rectangle around the selected elements based on where their edges fall. That's the space PowerPoint will use for alignment.

With multiple elements selected, you can choose to Align to Slide also, you just need to make that choice in the dropdown menu after you've selected those elements, and then reopen the dropdown menu to make your alignment decision.

You can also group elements using the Group dropdown in the Arrange section of the Shape Format tab. If you group elements together they act as if they are one element. So if I want a colored circle with text on it, I'd put in a shape for that circle and then a text box and I'd align the text box over the circle and then group the two together so that I can then move them together without worrying about them becoming misaligned. They'll also show as grouped in the Selection task pane.

Once you've grouped elements, you can use that same dropdown menu to ungroup them.

Charts

Okay, time to talk about charts.

Insert

You can insert a chart by clicking on the icon for Insert Chart in a presentation slide text box or by going to the Insert tab and choosing Chart from the Illustrations section.

What you will see with both choices is an Insert Chart dialogue box. Here you can see both options as well as the dialogue box:

I am not going to cover here the uses for the various types of charts. If you want to learn that, look to my Excel books where I do discuss how a column chart differs from a line chart and from a pie chart, etc. For this book, I'm going to assume you know what you're doing.

Click on the chart type you want and then click on OK.

PowerPoint will insert into your presentation slide a pre-populated chart that has fake data in it:

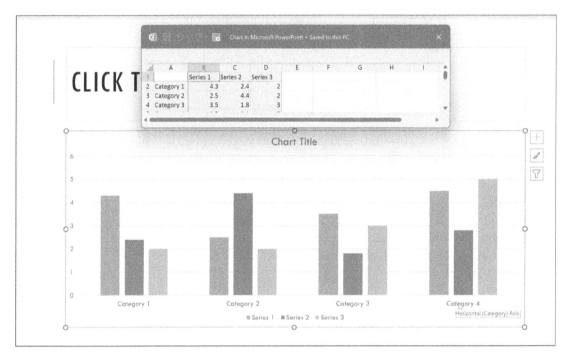

You can left-click and drag from the bottom corner of that Excel spreadsheet to see all of the data fields. Click into the Excel spreadsheet and enter your values to replace the fake ones. As you update the data, the chart on the presentation slide will also update:

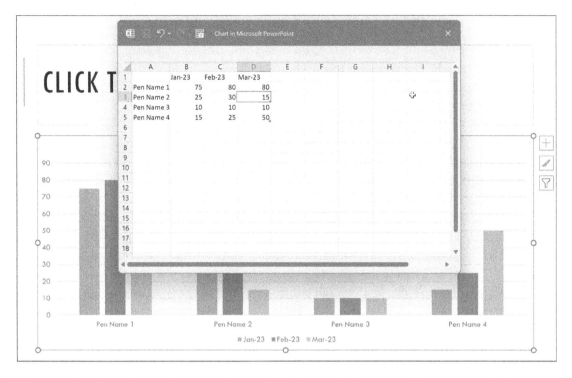

When you're done inputting your data, click the X in the top right corner of the Excel spreadsheet.

Edit Data

If you ever need to edit your data again, right-click on the chart, and choose Edit Data from the dropdown menu to bring up the Excel file again.

You can also go to the Chart Design tab and click on the Edit Data option in the Data section there.

Edit Appearance

The colors used in your chart should by default work with your chosen presentation theme but there may be other edits you want to make.

To edit the appearance of your chart, it works much the same way as it does in Excel so I'm going to cover this quickly. When you click on your chart, there will be a Chart Design tab with all of the standard design choices for a chart.

On the far left side is the Add Chart Element dropdown menu that lets you choose which elements to include on the chart such as axes, axis titles, chart title, data labels, etc.

Next to that are the Quick Layout options that combine various chart elements which can be useful if one is close to what you want.

After that is the Change Colors dropdown menu that uses color palettes that work for your presentation theme. So for mine, for example, it defaulted to shades of turquoise but there are some options in the Change Colors dropdown that use more greens than blues as well as some monochromatic choices.

Next to that is the Chart Styles section with different layouts for the chart that may work for you. (Again, I covered all of this in lots of detail in the Excel books, so if you really want to learn about working with charts in office programs, Excel is where you do that. There's even a specific book that's just for charts that's an extract from the intermediate Excel titles for each series.)

Finally, at the very end of that tab there is an option to change the chart type. Sometimes you may find that you don't want a bar chart but instead want a column chart or something like that. Easy enough to do. Just be careful when trying to move between non-compatible types of charts because that will not work well.

If those options don't give you enough control, then go to the Format tab. That will let you manually change the shape fill or shape outline for your chart elements. Click on the element first, and then make your formatting choice. (Honestly, you probably won't need to do this too often if you're working with a good theme, but it's there when needed.)

Edit Chart or Axes Titles

Most of your data labeling will happen in the Excel spreadsheet where you add your data, but that's not the case for things like your chart title or the titles of each axis. Those you have to manually input.

To do so, click on the text that reads "Chart Title" or "Axis Title" in the chart itself, use Ctrl + A to select all of the text that's currently there, and then type in your new text. Click away when done.

If you want to format that text in a way that it isn't already formatted, click there, Ctrl + A to select the text, and then use the Font section of the Home tab or the Text Fill dropdown menu in the WordArt Styles section of the Format tab. Either one will work.

Note that while you could get fancy with the formatting of a chart title and use WordArt Styles that have outlines and shadows and who knows what else, you probably shouldn't. It will likely interfere with the ability of your audience to read your text.

* * *

You can also double-click on your chart, or right-click and choose the Format Plot Area or similar Format X choice from the dropdown menu, to open the chart format task pane on the right-hand side of your workspace. That will include a variety of formatting options related to your chart. Use the first dropdown arrow to choose the type of formatting you want to do:

After that click through the various categories and options to find what you need.

Note that if you had a task pane open on the right-hand side already it may disappear and become an icon off to the side of this task pane. Like so:

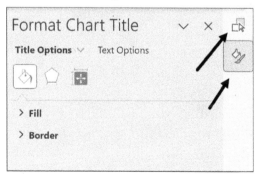

Here you can see that the Format Chart Title task pane is open but on the far right-hand side I have icons for that as well as the Selection task pane. If I click on that top icon it will switch over to the Selection task pane. If I click on the icon for Format Chart Title it will be hidden until I need it again.

Paste a Chart from Excel

Another option with PowerPoint is to build the chart in Microsoft Excel and then just treat it like a picture that you're copying from one program to another. Click on the chart in Excel, use Ctrl + C to copy, come back to PowerPoint, click on the slide where you want to paste the chart, and use Ctrl + V to paste.

When I just did that, the chart pasted in using the theme colors of my presentation in PowerPoint. I did have to click and drag from the corners to resize it to fit the space in the slide.

Also, when I chose to edit the data in that chart it opened the Excel file I had pulled the chart from. So don't copy an Excel chart from an Excel file unless that file will remain available in the same location or you have no intention of editing the chart.

Another option is to Paste Special - Picture. That will paste the chart in as a picture which means it will use the colors you used in Excel and you also won't be able to change anything on the chart at all.

Other Tips and Tricks

Rulers, Gridlines, and Guides

If you go to the Show section of the View tab there are checkboxes there for Ruler, Gridlines, and Guides.

Ruler will place a ruler along the top and left-hand side of your slide.

Guides by default will place dotted lines that run through the center point for the slide, so through the zero point on the ruler, although you can left-click and drag a guide line to a specific point on the ruler if you need to.

It's very hard to see, but here I have a line running across at the zero mark for the left-hand side, but I've moved the guideline for the top ruler over to 4. As you drag you'll see the value where the guideline is so you can know where you're lined up.

Having a guideline on your slide lets you manually position elements and make sure that they're aligned. This can allow you to keep positioning consistent across slides even when your elements are not left-aligned, right-aligned, or centered.

The final view option is to put gridlines over the entire slide that create one-inch by one-inch squares that you can also use for aligning elements:

The grid is built from the center of the slide outward, so the rectangles along the edges are not fully one-inch square.

Neither guidelines nor gridlines will be visible on the presentation. They're just there for you to use as you prepare your document.

Equations

If you lecture using mathematical equations then the Symbols section of the Insert tab will provide a lot of help for you. Click on the dropdown menu for Equation to see some common equations such as the Area of a Circle. Or go to the bottom of the dropdown and click on Insert New Equation or Ink Equation.

Insert New Equation will open an Equation tab for you that has all of the elements of an equation. Click on them to build your equation. Use the Structures section for some common structures such as a fraction. The boxes for each equation component can then be clicked on to add specific values like x, y, a number or another equation component.

Ink Equation lets you write your math into a field and then PowerPoint will convert that to an equation for you. This probably works best if you have a stylus, but it just managed to decipher my very poorly-done writing of 2+2 using my mouse.

Esc to exit if you need to.

WordArt

We have briefly seen the WordArt option more than once as we've been walking through the various elements you can insert into a slide. WordArt can also be found in the Text section of the Insert tab. Click on the dropdown arrow there to see various formatting choices that are pre-populated.

If you click on one of those options, PowerPoint will insert a text box that says, "Your text here" with text that is formatted that way. It will also bring up a Shape Format tab that has the WordArt Styles section:

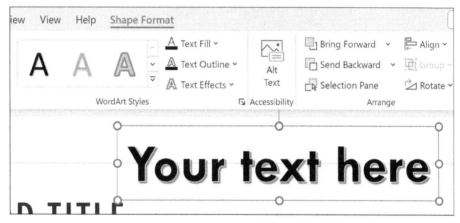

In addition to the twenty pre-formatted options available in that section, you can change the Text Fill color and the Text Outline color to anything you want. In the Text Effects dropdown menu you can choose Shadow, Reflection, Glow, Bevel, 3-D Rotation, or Transform options.

I do know a few people who have used PowerPoint over the years to design book covers. In those instances, these settings can be very useful. So I'm mentioning them, but not focusing on them, because in a basic business presentation, WordArt should be used sparingly or not at all.

Other Text Formatting

I covered most text formatting options in the first book in this series, but there were a few I left out. Three are available in the Font section of the Home tab:

The first one there, that looks like a blurry S is text shadowing which will put a shadow behind your text.

The next one, which looks like an a and a b with a line through them is strikethrough which will put a strikethrough across a line of text.

The third one there in that bottom row is character spacing and it has a dropdown menu because there are choices for very tight, tight, normal, loose, and very loose.

Here are examples of all three of the above:

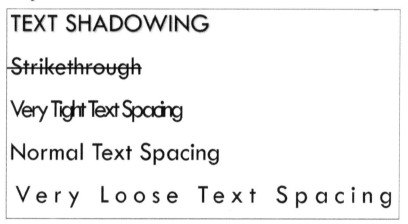

There are also a few additional options in the Font dialogue box. Select your text and then click on the expansion arrow in the bottom right corner of the Font section of the Home tab, or right-click and choose Font from the dropdown menu to see that dialogue box.

The additional choices available here are Double Strikethrough, Superscript, Subscript, Small Caps, and All Caps.

Symbols

If you ever need to insert a symbol into your presentation, you can do so using the Symbol option in the Symbols section of the Insert tab. Click on that to open the Symbol dialogue box. Find the symbol you want and double-click on it or click on it once and then click on Insert at the bottom of the dialogue box.

The Symbol dialogue box will stay open after it inserts your symbol for you. Click on the X in the top right corner to close it when you're done.

Symbols can be formatted with colors, font size, etc. just like text.

Format Slide Background

If you're working with a presentation theme, chances are you won't need to do this, but if you ever do need to change the background color on a slide or series of slides, go to the Customize section of the Design tab and click on Format Background.

This will open the Format Background task pane where you can then choose from a solid fill, gradient fill, picture or texture fill, or pattern fill. You can also choose a color and a degree of transparency. This will fill the entire slide but behind any elements on that slide.

Here, for example, I added a striped background to this slide but it only shows in the space behind the photo:

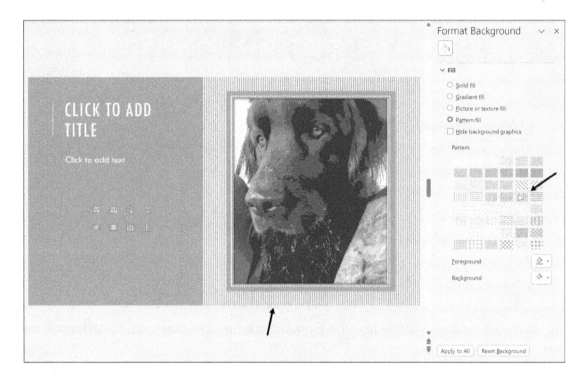

Format Background or Perimeter of Text Box

You can also change the background in a text box by right-clicking on that element and choosing the Format Shape option. It will open the Format Shape task pane where you have choices for solid fill, etc. as well as no fill for that text box. If you choose an option other than no fill there will be options for color and transparency as well.

This is also where you can add a solid-colored or gradient line around the perimeter of the text box using the options under Line.

Import From Word

It is possible to write an outline in Word that you then import into PowerPoint where each new section of the outline becomes a new slide and then the subpoints of the outline are the bullet points on the slide. To make it work, you need to use the Heading styles for each level of your outline when you create it in Word.

Once you have the outline, save it, and then go to the Slides section of the Home tab in PowerPoint, click on the dropdown under New Slide, and choose Slides from Outline. Navigate to where you saved the Word file and choose it. PowerPoint will then convert that outline into a presentation for you.

Select All

To select all of the objects on a page or all of the text in a text box use Ctrl + A. What is actually selected will depend on where your cursor was or was not at the time you used the shortcut. If text is selected it will be shaded gray. If elements are selected you'll see white circles around their edges. You can also click into the slides task pane and select all the slides there using Ctrl + A.

There is also a Select dropdown available in the Editing section of the Home tab which has options for Select All, Select Objects, and Selection Pane.

Slide Transitions

In the last book we discussed how to have different elements on a slide appear at different times. There are also options for creating special transitions between slides.

I have seen this used very effectively, but most of the time it is not, so exercise caution.

Click on the thumbnail of the slide you want to transition *to* in the left-hand task pane, go to the Transitions tab, and then click on the transition type you want to use from the Transition To This Slide set of options.

You can use the Preview option in the Transitions tab to see what the transition will look like.

To control how long the transition takes, adjust the value in the Timing section of the Transitions tab. You can also control if the transition requires a mouse click or is set to automatically happen after a set period of time from that section. And if there's a sound that should play at the same time.

The one time I saw this very effectively used was in a presentation that was running before a talk on prisoner abuse where the presentation had been set up to move from one image of prisoner abuse to another every five seconds or so. I think it was also paired with a ticking sound. It really made those images hit home and set the stage for the talk (which was about the psychology of evil). So this can be done well and does have uses. Just maybe be careful about using it in a normal business presentation just to have each slide appear in a different way.

Master Slides

I consider master slides an advanced-level topic, because changes made to master slides impact all of the slides in a presentation and so messing around in there is a very good way to screw it all up real fast.

But I started at a new employer recently and someone had really messed things up in the corporate template. As in, I couldn't make a multi-level bulleted list no matter what I did. Because this person had gone into the master slide and limited it to one bullet level. I don't think they meant to, but that's what they did.

So I want to at least let you know where to look if you run into this sort of issue.

You can see your master slides by going to the View tab and clicking on Slide Master under Master Views. Here's the first few master slides for the theme I've been using throughout this book:

Any change to that top slide will impact all of the other master slides in the theme as well as every single slide in the presentation. A change to one of the other slides below that will just impact slides that use that layout.

Here's what a master slide looks like:

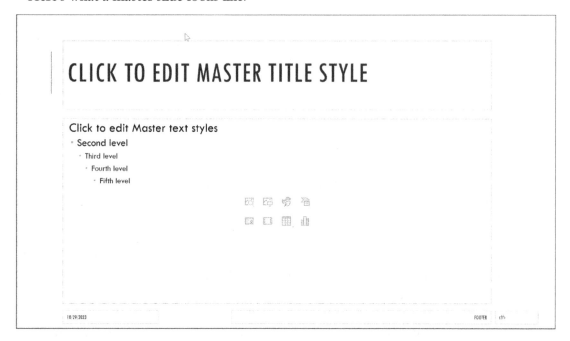

See that list of bulleted items there that goes down to a fifth level? If you want to have a five-level bulleted list, it needs to show that way in the master slide. That's the issue I had at my new employer. Whoever built the template stopped at the first-level bullet.

You can edit a master slide to change the appearance of your slides.

So, say for example, I don't like that the first level of text in this slide has no bullet. I could go into the top master slide and change that.

But I really would recommend exercising caution here. Because that change will impact every single slide in the presentation. Perhaps in a negative way.

In my opinion, the best thing to do is choose a good presentation theme up front that has addressed all of this and then just live with the choices they made when they created it.

But in case you need it, that's where you find it. Just maybe save a backup copy first before you start mucking around in there?

To exit the master slide view, click on Close Master View in the top menu.

Sections

If you have a really long presentation, consider inserting sections into the presentation. When you have sections you can then collapse them so that it's easier to navigate through the slides in the left-hand side of your workspace. You can also click and drag to move an entire section at once if needed and can print that section of slides easily.

To create a new section, right-click onto the space in the left-hand navigation pane that is directly above the slide that you want to have start your new section. So not on the slide itself, but in the gray space around it. Choose Add Section from the dropdown menu:

A Rename Section dialogue box will pop up and let you name the section. Type in the name you want and then click on Rename.

If you add sections, you sort of need to commit to using them throughout the presentation, because all slides from that point forward will be assigned to that section.

Once you've inserted a section, you can click on the arrow to the left of the section name to collapse the section and hide all slides in that section. If it's already collapsed, click there to expand it.

Here I've created four sections and you can see that for the three sections at the top that are collapsed (Default Section, Tables, and Picture Videos SmartArt) it shows the number of slides in each section. For the section that is not collapsed, Charts, it just shows the slides:

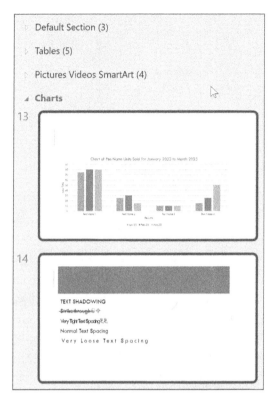

To rename or remove a section later, right-click on the section name:

You can choose to rename the section, remove the section, remove all sections, or remove that section as well as its slides. There are also options in that dropdown to collapse or expand all sections at once.

To move a section, either use the Move Section Up or Move Section Down options in that dropdown, or left-click the section name and drag until the section is where you want it. When you move a section that will move all slides in that section as well.

It is possible to include a link to a section of slides from another slide. Click and drag the section name onto that slide. That will let you jump in your presentation to that set of slides before you then come back to the original slide and continue on with your presentation.

When you do this, it will embed a small image of the first slide in the section onto that other slide. When presenting, just click on that image and it will make it full-size and then let you move through the slides of that section before once more minimizing the image and returning to the first slide.

Comments

PowerPoint doesn't have a track changes function like Word does. The next best option is to use Comments rather than do something like [have we verified this number] in the middle of the text on a slide. Typing text that should not be there onto a slide is a good way to embarrass yourself when it comes time to present.

So use comments if you have something to say when reviewing a presentation.

To insert a comment, click onto that point in the presentation and then go to the Review tab and click on New Comment. That will open the Comments task pane on the right-hand side of the workspace:

In the "start a conversation" field, type whatever you want to say. Use Ctrl + Enter to finalize the comment or click on the bright orangeish arrow.

Below each comment that's added, there will be a Reply field. Click into that to add any response to the original comment. You can also just click on the little thumbs up sign to like someone else's comment.

Click on the three dots on the right-hand side of the comment for options to delete the thread or mark it as resolved. Here we have one comment with a response, the next one with a thumbs up, and you can see the options to delete or resolve that comment:

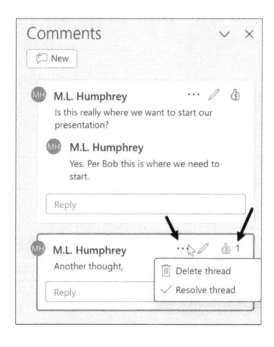

Comments do not show on the presentation itself. But if there are comments and you click on that slide they will appear in the Comment task pane.

If you want a note on the slide itself, choose the Show Comments dropdown in the Comments section of the Review tab and select Show Advanced Markup.

You can also use the Comments section of the Review tab to navigate to the previous or next comment. The Delete option in that section allows you to delete that one comment, delete all comments on the slide, or delete all comments in the presentation.

Save As Other Formats

I already covered in the introductory book in this series the basics of saving a PowerPoint file, but now I want to cover two special cases, saving as a PDF and saving as an image.

As a reminder, to save a file as a different format you need to go to the File tab and click on Save As. There is a dropdown menu on that Save As screen that will then let you choose the file format you want:

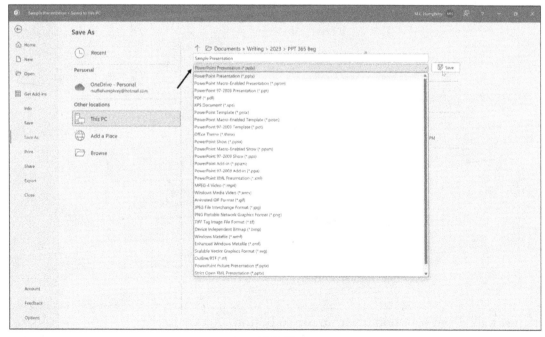

PDF

Depending on your available programs, you may actually have a Save as PDF option on the left-hand side that you can click on if you want a PDF file. That saves a step and will immediately bring up a dialogue box where you can choose your location and file name.

But for us mere mortals without that fancy set-up, click on Save As, and then in the dropdown menu for format choose PDF from the list. For me right now it's the fourth one down.

When I chose that, PowerPoint brought up an option about investigating accessibility. I am going to ignore it for now. We'll cover accessibility in a moment.

If you like the name for the document and the current location, just click on Save. If not, click into the name field and change it or click on Browse to navigate to a new location for the file.

You could have also started with the Browse option and changed the Save As Type in the dropdown menu in that Save As dialogue box to PDF. That's another way to do it.

Either way, click Save when you have the name, location, and file type set. Your PowerPoint will save with default settings, which means one slide per page and just the slide.

If you want more control over what you are turning into a PDF, click on Browse to bring up the Save As dialogue box, change the type to PDF, and then click on Options in the bottom section of the dialogue box to open the Options dialogue box:

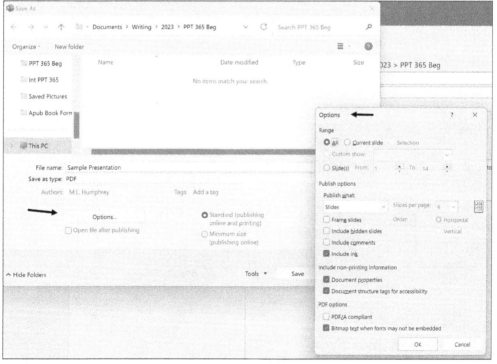

Let's just walk down your options from top to bottom.

First up, you can choose to print all slides, the current slide, a selection of slides (but you have to do that before you choose to print), or a range of slides (but you have to know before you choose to print what the slide range you want is).

For non-continuous slides, so say slides 4, 10, and 12, you'd use selection and hold down the Ctrl key as you clicked on each one you wanted in the main workspace before coming to Save As.

Next, you can choose to print the slides which will put each slide in your presentation on one page in landscape format. Your other options there are to print handouts, note pages, or an outline view, just like we discussed in the introductory book of this series for printing. You can also set here the number of slides to print per page.

Keep in mind this will be "printed" to a PDF file.

Next there are checkboxes to add a frame around your slides, to include any hidden slides from the presentation, to include comments added to any slide, and to include ink that was added to the slide.

After that you can choose whether to include the document properties and any document structure tags for accessibility.

Essentially all of those are print settings but applied to saving your PDF.

Finally, you can choose whether to make your PDF compliant with the PDF/A standard and whether to turn fonts that can't be embedded into the presentation into bitmap text. If you're just printing your slides as handouts, don't worry about these last two at all. That is more for when you need the PDF to upload somewhere, like a publication site.

* * *

Another option for creating a PDF is to go to File and then use the Export option instead and choose Create PDF/XPS Document. That will bring up a Publish as PDF or XPS dialogue box. Just make sure your Save As type is PDF. It should be by default.

(As a side note, I once had an analyst turn documents into XPS files instead of PDF and the recipient of those files lost their mind over it, so only use XPS if it's for you or you have already confirmed with the other party that they can handle XPS files. That was not a fun afternoon for me.)

Image Files

Early on when I was writing the first versions of these books and I needed images that had labels on them, I used PowerPoint to do that. I took my screenshot, dropped the image into a slide on PowerPoint and then added arrows and text boxes to label what needed labeled.

In order to be able to then use that in a book I had to export the slides as images. Not the best or easiest way to do that, but it worked. So if you ever need something similar or have another reason for turning your slides into image files, you can do that.

To do so, go to File, Save As, and choose the type of image file you want from the Save As Type dropdown.

The most common type of image files people want is usually JPEG File Interchange Format (.jpg) or PNG Portable Network Graphics Format (.png).

If you're doing something like this book, though, use TIFF Tag Image File Format (.tif) instead. Don't ask me why now, but I went down a very long rabbit hole over this and ultimately something about lossless compression and image integrity blah, blah, blah led me to decide that for the non-fiction books I publish .tif is the best format. Probably more because of the ebooks than the print books, though.

Anyway. Make your choice and click on Save.

PowerPoint is then going to bring up a dialogue box that asks "Which Slides Do You Want to Export?" and give you the choice between All Slides and Just This One. You can also choose Cancel.

The way this works is that PowerPoint will take each individual slide and turn it into an image for you. So if you choose All Slides and you have a hundred slides in that presentation, it will create a hundred image files for you. They will all be saved into a folder that uses the presentation name. Like so:

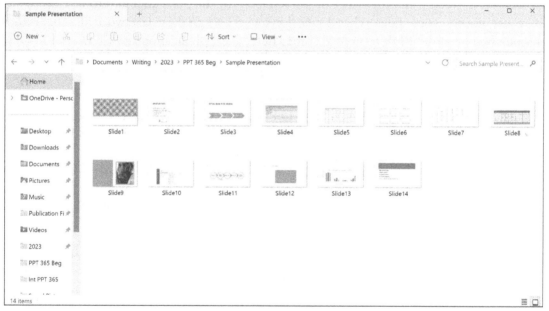

See how each image of a slide is named Slide 1, Slide 2, etc. based on the order in the presentation.

Even if you try to select just a subset of slides, your choices will still only be All or One.

If you choose to save just one slide instead, PowerPoint will save that one slide as an image using the name you provided in the Save As screen. Remember it is only that one image, not all of them. So even if it has a name like "Sample Presentation", it will still just be an image of that one slide.

(Maybe that's obvious to you, but the first time I tried this it was not in fact obvious to me.)

GIF

You can use the animated gif choice in the dropdown to create a little animation of your entire presentation that will walk through from start to finish with all of your transitions and videos, etc. But if you're going to use this option, you really should review the timing of the various transitions in your slide to make sure it's slow enough for people to follow. By default mine really was not.

Accessibility

PowerPoint now has a lot of accessibility tools built in that you can use. It will tell you when you don't have alternative text on an image or when a color choice isn't going to work for all members of an audience.

To see the accessibility choices, go to the Accessibility section of the Review tab. There is a dropdown menu there for Check Accessibility that has a number of options: Check Accessibility, Alt Text, Reading Order Pane, etc:

Click on Check Accessibility to see the Accessibility task pane with various suggestions:

You can click on the arrow for each one to expand it and see where the error is and then click on that item to go to that point in the presentation. PowerPoint will also explain to you what the issue is. So here it says that the contrast between my white text and that turquoise background may be hard to read:

I don't necessarily agree. But if I did, when I click on that item it also shows me the Change Colors option so that I can immediately go and fix that without having to search around for how to do so.

The bigger your audience, probably the more you should pay attention to these alerts. Especially pay attention to errors related to color blindness for a visual presentation because about 8% of men have some form of color blindness.

For presentations that you're going to post online for someone to read through, then alt text becomes more important for your images.

Anyway. Something to consider to reach a wider audience with your presentation. You can also click on the Accessibility: Investigate option at the bottom left of your workspace to open that task pane if you don't want to go to the Accessibility tab.

Conclusion

Alright. That's it for this book. There are still things you can do in PowerPoint that we did not cover, but at this point you should be perfectly capable of putting together a nice, solid PowerPoint presentation that incorporates images, videos, SmartArt, etc.

Of course, the world is unpredictable so who knows what will come up in the future that you need to know. Good news is that Microsoft has very good help available.

If there's something specific that you want to know about, often the easiest way to learn more is to hold your mouse over that option and see if there is a Tell Me More choice:

Click on that if there is. It will open the Help task pane on the right-hand side of the workspace to provide help for that specific topic:

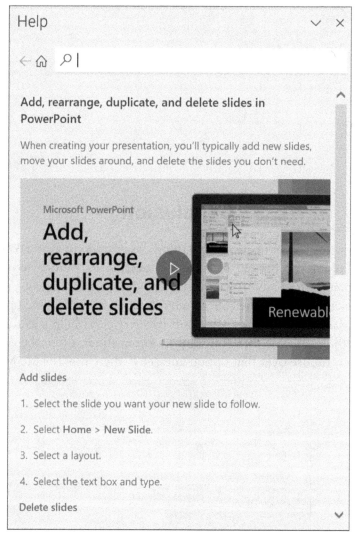

Depending on the topic, there will be descriptive text or maybe a video like in this case.

If there isn't a Tell Me More option to click on, you can also just go to the Help tab and click on Help there to open the task pane and then search for the topic you want to know more about.

If you just want general training, the Show Training option under the Help tab will bring up various topics that you can click on to see more information.

If all else fails, search the internet. I like to search using "PowerPoint 365" and then the topic I'm interested in. I try to look for the microsoft support results.

One final note, under that Help tab there is a What's New option. Click on that to get the New Features and Updates link in the right-hand task pane. This will let you see recent changes to PowerPoint 365 as well as upcoming changes.

If you're going to use 365 programs you have to accept that they may change on you without much control on your end. On one hand, that's great, you always have the latest and greatest. On another hand it sucks, because you get used to how something works and then maybe you walk in one day and it's all different. (Or you're writing a book on PowerPoint and someone just randomly decides to change the default options in the text box of a slide without notice, making your book instantly out of date.)

And the changes aren't in my opinion as fully vetted as when they do a big formal new product release. I just clicked on that link and there were changes made on September 28, October 10, October 25, and October 31. The changes to PowerPoint were mostly error fixes, but when you're updating things on a rolling, ongoing basis like that sometimes bad things slip through. Or you get something that's half-baked and they want users to give them free feedback to finalize it.

So 365 programs are probably going to be a little more buggy than working in a fixed version, like PowerPoint 2019, but the fixes that are needed will probably happen faster. Which is why knowing how to use Help and checking for what's new are both good skills to have when working in 365.

Okay. Real quick. What didn't we cover that you may still need to know?

I didn't cover working in Teams, so if you are in an organization that uses Teams, you may want to explore how that works. I also didn't cover how to Record a presentation. If you need that, check out the Record tab. I didn't go into full detail about the accessibility options. I didn't cover the various View choices you have. Nor did I cover Macros or Drawing tools.

That's because these books are geared towards the average user who has average needs. You may need more. But hopefully you now have that solid foundation to work from so that it's easy to go and find what you need.

If you get stuck, feel free to reach out. I don't check my email daily, but I do check it and will help if I can. Some of the items I didn't cover are because in twenty-five years I've never needed them but I'm happy to find help resources for you if you can't find them or try it myself and see what issues I run into.

Finally, I've said this before but I want to say it again: Always keep in mind what your goal is with your presentation. Don't add bells and whistles unless they support that goal. And remember that the more you put on a slide in terms of text, the less your audience is going to be paying attention to you. That's just human nature.

Alright, then. Good luck with it.

Index

About the Author

M.L. Humphrey is a former stockbroker with a degree in Economics from Stanford and an MBA from Wharton who has spent close to twenty years as a regulator and consultant in the financial services industry.

You can reach M.L. at mlhumphreywriter@gmail.com or at mlhumphrey.com.